BRAVE HEARTS REBEL SPIRITS

A Spiritual Activists Handbook

Brooke Shelby Biggs

ANITA RODDICK BOOKS

Anita Roddick Books
An Imprint of Anita Roddick Publications, Ltd.
93 East Street
Chichester
West Sussex
England PO19 1HA
www.AnitaRoddick.com

ISBN: 0-9543959-0-5

Publishing Director: Cal Joy
Consulting Publishing Director: Justine Roddick
Communications Director: Karen Bishop
Author: Brooke Shelby Biggs
Editor: Kate McKinley
Cover Design: Steve Chambers, Kevin Newman
Design: Wheelhouse Creative, Ltd.
www.WheelhouseCreative.co.uk
Photo Illustration: Steve Chambers
Photography Research: Cal Joy, Steve Chambers

Printed on Recycled Paper

Printed in the United States

A catalogue record for this book is available from the British
Library.

Distributed in the United Kingdom by Airlift Book Company
www.Airlift.co.uk

Special thanks to John Owen, Terry Newell and Chris
Hemesath from Weldon Owen, for their kindness and
generosity in producing this book. www.weldonowen.com

**Red
Wheel**

Distributed in North America by Red Wheel/Weiser Books
www.RedWheelWeiser.com

Library of Congress Cataloging-in-Publication Data.
Brave Hearts, Rebel Spirits
ISBN: 0-9543959-0-5

03 10 9 8 7 6 5 4 3 2 1

DEDICATION

THIS BOOK IS DEDICATED TO ALL THOSE UNCELEBRATED HELL-RAISERS, TRUTH-TELLERS, AND RISK-TAKERS WHO HAVE LIVED WHAT THEY BELIEVE WITH SUCH GRACE, HONOR, AND COURAGE. NOT ALL OF THEM COULD FIT INSIDE THIS BOOK, SO THIS BOOK IS, INSTEAD, A GIFT TO THEM...

...it is for Kimberly Bobo, Mike Rankin, Alan Watson Featherstone, Aung San Suu Kyi, Mililani Trask, Trevor Huddleston, the Sisters of El Salvador, Leonard Peltier, Fannie Lou Hamer, Ella Baker, Helen Prejean, Palden Gyatso, Bernie Glassman, Ma Jaya Sati Bhagavati, Black Elk, Leonardo Boff, Ken Saro-Wiwa, Ghassan Andoni, Petra Kelly, Rosalie Little Thunder, Mary Ann Finch, Bishop Carlos Felipe Ximenes Belo, Terry Greenblatt, Bruno Hussar, Lobsang Dhargyal, Jim Lawson, John Lewis, Harriet Tubman, Vimala Thakar, Ricardo Falla, Badshan Khan, Uri Avnery, Vikas Singh, Zafaryab Ahmed, Zia Mian, A. Philip Randolph, Adele Kirsten, Jimmy and Rosalyn Carter, Gustavo Gutierrez, Robert McAffe Brown, Nirmala Deshpande, Ibrahim Ramey, Rebecca Adamson, John Dear, Ingrid Washinawatok...

...and so very many more.

Anita Roddick

Anita Roddick OBE
Founder of The Body Shop

1

CONTENTS

Dedication   1
Contents   2
Introduction   4

CHAPTER ONE: FUGITIVES FROM INJUSTICE
Daniel and Philip Berrigan   **Catholic Priests, Anti-War Activists**   10
Trident Ploughshares   British Interfaith Peace Activists   28
Dorothy Day   Founder, Catholic Worker Movement   31

CHAPTER TWO: DIVINE OBEDIENCE
Father Roy Bourgeois   **Catholic Priest, Founder of**   36
                                 The School of the Americas Watch
Dorothy Hennessey   Catholic Nun, SOA Watch Activist   48
Martin Sheen   Catholic Actor and Activist   50
Oscar Romero   Archbishop of El Salvador   52

CHAPTER THREE: THE RADICAL HUMANIST
John Trudell   **Santee Sioux Indigeneous Right Activist**   58
Rigoberta Menchu   Mayan Indigenous Rights Activist   73
Winona LaDuke   Ojibwe Environmental and Indigenous Rights Activist   76

CHAPTER FOUR: A SPARK FOR JUSTICE
Isabell Coe   **Wiragariee, Aboriginal Tent Embassy Diplomat**   80
Charles Perkins   Arrente Aboriginal Civil-Rights Advocate   92
Kevin Buzzacott   Arabunna Elder, Anti-Nuclear Activist   96

CHAPTER FIVE: THE AMERICAN GANDHI
A.J.Muste   **Calvinist Quaker Labor Leader.**   104
Cesar Chavez   Founder, United Farm Workers   118
Mother Jones   Catholic Labor Agitator   122

CHAPTER SIX: THE KING OF KINDNESS

Vinoba Bhave	**Brahman Land-Rights Leader**	**128**
Satish Kumar	Jain Monk, Walker for Peace	138
Vandana Shiva	Hindu Anti-Globalization Activist	143

CHAPTER SEVEN: TRUTH IN LOVE, RELENTLESSLY

Mel White	**Evangelical Christian Gay Rights Advocate**	**150**
Jose Cabezon	Buddhist Gay Liberationist	166
Bayard Rustin	Quaker Civil Rights Organizer	168

CHAPTER EIGHT: SHALOM, SALAM

Neta Golan	**Buddhist Jew, Middle East Peace Activist**	**176**
Jean Zaru	Quaker Palestinian Peace Advocate	192
Thich Nhat Hanh	Buddhist Monk, Peace Worker	196
Meena Keshwar Kamal	Muslim Founder of the Association of the Women of Afghanistan	199

CHAPTER NINE: HOPE AND RESISTANCE

Janusz Korczak	**Jewish Child Advocate**	**204**
Dietrich Bonhoeffer	Protestant Theologian, Nazi Resister	218
Mairead Maguire	Catholic Peace Organizer	220

CHAPTER TEN: MAN OF THE TREES

Richard St. Barbe Baker	**Baha'i Conservationist**	**228**
Julia Butterfly Hill	Pantheist Environmentalist	240
Roads Protesters	Pagan Earth Defenders	242
Sulak Sivaraksa	Buddhist Environmental Organizer	244

Acknowledgments	248
Photography Credits	250
More From Anita Roddick Publishing	252

INTRODUCTION

BY ANITA RODDICK OBE

Here's a challenge: Name 10 tyrants, despots, or dictators who have wrought havoc and misery on the world. No problem, right? Now (without skipping ahead in this book!) name 10 spiritual leaders who have been courageous, inspirational, and changed others' lives for the better even at the cost of their own. I fear most of us cannot. It's a sign of our times that the world is so obsessed with and preoccupied by the bad that we spend little time focused on the good.

That imbalance has helped fuel an amazing resurgence in people's hunger for spiritual enlightenment (and spawned vast industries to separate the yearning from their cash). We seek hope and meaning now because we have come to live in a world in which a perverse profusion of economic values has superseded every other human value, including peace and compassion.

At the same time, our spiritual institutions have often failed us; instead of a tool for peace and a vehicle for understanding the world and each other, modern-day institutionalized religion is often wielded as a weapon of oppression. Too many proselytizers use fear and intimidation instead of joy and celebration to keep the faithful close and malleable. There is more sermonizing on sin and evil than on the things that truly matter, like love, honesty, kindness, and fairness.

Thankfully, as in almost all things, it has been the rebels among the faithful who have shown the way back into the light. And these are the people who helped shape my thinking about the world from my earliest years. In fact, my worldview was first and most powerfully shaped by two Catholic women, one a saint to the world, the other a saint to me.

Sister Immaculata, a teacher in my convent school in the South of England taught us the power of language. Every day we prepared tea and beds in a room in St. Joseph's Convent set aside for "tramps," the term we used to refer to the homeless in those days. But Sister Immaculata banned the word. Instead, she insisted we call these men "Knights of the Road." And in keeping with a kind of Catholic morality that seems out of fashion in some parts of the Church today, we were also being taught that service to the weak and the frail was part of our moral education, and that education or knowledge without action was no education at all.

The other saint was Joan of Arc, whose story gave me my moral imagination. My first heroine, she stood up for something in a way that set my mind reeling: She fought against the false gods of conformity and apathy. More than anything, as a child, I wanted a little bit of her to live in me.

As I grew, I came to respect and admire other spiritual rebels and leaders, like Jesus, Martin Luther King, Mahatma Gandhi, Nelson Mandela, and the Dalai Lama. They applied their abstract spiritual traditions to the world around them, with the most profound and moving results. They put their bodies on the line and they got their hands dirty, rejecting an easier path. None of them were proselytizers, each simply lived his beliefs actively, bravely, boldly, and in many cases, downright radically.

This book is an attempt to lift these spiritual activists, religious changemakers, and soulful rebels into the spotlight alongside their iconic forerunners. I feel strongly that the people featured in this book should become as familiar to us as Mother Teresa, that we should have an army of spiritual leaders in our knowledge bank who inspire us to be a little braver and bolder.

This book is more anthology than compendium, as of course it could only hold a small number of those whose work qualifies them for a place within its pages. We have tried to make the collection reflect the geographical, spiritual, and political diversity of this far-flung bunch of radical believers, selecting those with the most compelling and inspirational stories we found on our journey of discovery.

In the spirit of recognizing all the worthy people who did not find their way into this modest book, I invite you, the reader, to nominate your own "brave souls and rebel spirits" on the companion Web site at AnitaRoddick.com.

ANITA RODDICK, 2003

FUGITIVES

FROM

INJUSTICE

PHILIP AND DANIEL BERRIGAN

CATHOLIC PRIESTS, ANTI-WAR ACTIVISTS

Radical Josephite priest Philip Berrigan stands in front of a slightly open file cabinet, staring solemnly into the breast pocket of his trenchcoat. Moments after this grainy photograph was snapped in October 1967, Philip pulled a vial of blood—a mixture of animal blood and his own—out of the pocket and poured its contents over dozens of draft files.

Philip and three of his friends—Tom Lewis, David Eberhardt, and James Mengel—had walked calmly into Baltimore's Selective Service office that morning, and asked to look at their own draft files. They spread out, each at a different file cabinet, and silently, serenely, opened a drawer and poured in a vial of blood.

As they waited for their arrest, the group passed out Bibles and politely explained to onlookers and dumbfounded draft board employees that the blood symbolized that of American soldiers and Vietnamese, as well as the blood of Christ.

That action marked the genesis of a remarkable phenomenon: the American Catholic nonviolent, direct-action anti-war movement. That day, Philip became the first priest in America to be arrested for an act of civil disobedience. He would not be the last; indeed, he

ACT NOW www.plowsharesactions.org

"Civil disobedience has always been the recourse of people of conscience, of people facing overwhelming power and needing to awaken their fellow citizens to action." —Howard Zinn

Philip (left) and Daniel Berrigan

opened the floodgates of religious anti-war activism. Within a year both he and his brother Daniel, a Jesuit priest and poet, would top the FBI's Ten Most Wanted list and appear simultaneously on the covers of *Newsweek* and *Time*. Over the next 35 years, the two, between them, would spend nearly two decades in jail and garner two Nobel Peace Prize nominations, all for nonviolent protest against war.

BORN REVOLUTIONARIES

The six Berrigan boys were raised in a working-class Midwestern American town by their Catholic parents. Their father, Tom Berrigan, was second-generation Irish, and a proud union man. When the Catholic Church instructed the faithful to foreswear union membership in the 1930s on the grounds that unions represented godless socialism, Tom turned his back on the Church. Still, his six sons all attended parochial school, and his wife, Freda, a devout German-Catholic immigrant, raised the boys in the faith. Daniel, born in 1920, was the first to choose the priesthood, entering a strict Jesuit seminary directly out of high school. He spent nearly 20 years studying theology in seclusion and contemplation, and much of the rest of his adult life was spent in academia.

Philip, born in 1923, was drafted after one semester of college, and did a tour of combat duty in Europe during World War II. When he returned, he was drinking heavily, disturbed by the violence he had seen in Europe and the racism he witnessed at home in boot camp in the Deep South. Soon enough, Philip too entered a seminary, but a Jospehite one. The Josephites were dedicated to the cause of racial equality and their ministries served underprivileged black communities in urban areas. Philip was quickly swept up in the civil-rights movement: He attended desegregation marches, participated in bus boycotts and sit-ins, and corresponded with Martin Luther King, Jr. Like many Christian pacifists, Philip believed that justice and peace were inextricably linked, and one simply could not be achieved without the other. It was only natural for him to apply his passion for civil rights to the anti-war effort when the United States invaded Vietnam.

Of the two, Philip was the firebrand and risk-taker; Daniel was more cautious and thoughtful. Philip spent a decade working in the slums and ghettos and marching with civil-rights leaders; Daniel spent most of 20 years in contemplation. The brothers came together, and, with Trappist monk and famed theologian Thomas Merton, founded an interfaith coalition against the war and wrote to major American newspapers arguing their spiritual opposition to the war in intellectual terms. But Philip began to chafe—he wanted to be on the ground, in the streets, doing something, not just writing about hating the war, but actively getting in the way of the war machine itself.

After Philip's arrest in Baltimore, Daniel began to consider Philip's new tactics. In early 1968, a remarkable opportunity arose. Howard Zinn, an academic and anti-war activist, invited Daniel to join him on a mission to Hanoi to broker the release of three American pilots who had been taken prisoner by the North Vietnamese. When they alerted U.S. military officials of their mission and itinerary, the government refused to sanction the trip, and FBI director J. Edgar Hoover denounced them as traitors. U.S. war planes repeatedly dropped bombs where their envoy was scheduled to be. The three airmen were eventually brought home—the first POWs released from North Vietnam and returned unharmed. But Zinn and Berrigan received no acknowledgment from the Air Force or the Nixon administration.

CATONSVILLE

That experience radicalized Daniel and moved him, as his brother had urged, from dissent to active resistance. Philip was adamant that the Baltimore action must be repeated at draft boards around the country. It had to become a movement, repeated on an ever-larger scale, not just one symbolic act. Already Philip had assembled eight people, priests and nuns among them, for a more daring foray into a draft board. He asked Daniel to join them. After a night of thought, Daniel agreed.

"[I had] a sense, as I recall, of immense freedom," Daniel writes in his autobiography, *To Dwell in Peace* (Harper and Row, 1987). "As though in choosing, I could now breathe deep and call my life my own...and suddenly my heart lifted and I knew." This, and all the Berrigans' future actions would be guided by a simple ethic, which they say is dictated by the Bible itself: No principle is worth the loss of a single human life, and any government property connected to the destruction of life is by this definition illegitimate. "Some property has no right to exist," Daniel insists.

ACT NOW www.plowsharesactions.org

By the spring of 1968, Napalm was being used in Indochina as an incendiary agent dropped from airplanes, ostensibly to thin the jungle and raze suspected enemy hideouts. In fact, it was often used to incinerate entire villages, including their civilian populations. In addition to widespread destruction, Napalm also had the horrifying effect of clinging to the skin of humans in its path. Pictures of horribly burned peasants began emerging from South East Asia, bringing the stark reality of modern war and human "collateral damage" to American television sets.

Philip seized on the idea of Napalm as the perfect symbolic sequel to blood. A local high school physics teacher helped concoct the explosive using

Vietnamese child burned by Napalm

a recipe from a Green Beret handbook. It was quickly done: two parts kerosene, one part soap flakes. The next morning, the group divided up the mixture, tucked cans of it under their jackets, and headed for the Selective Service Board in the sleepy suburb of Catonsville, Maryland. They tipped off some local media to assemble in the parking lot.

When they arrived, three of the raiders calmly walked through the doors and announced their intention to remove and destroy files, which Philip described as "hunting licenses against humans." None of the secretaries looked up. The remaining six participants brought in wire trash bins and began emptying file cabinets. They began with the 1-A files—the first in line to be drafted into military service and sent to Vietnam. When they finished, there were 378 files jammed in the trash bins. Still calm, the group walked back out into the parking lot, set the baskets down, doused them with their homemade Napalm, and set the whole mess alight with a cigarette butt. The nine raiders—all of them Catholic, Philip and Daniel in their clerical collars—solemnly gathered around the blaze and bowed their heads in prayer.

Daniel spoke: "Our apologies, good friends, for the fracture of good order, the burning of paper instead of children... We could not, so help us God, do otherwise... We say: killing is disorder, life and gentleness and community and unselfishness is the only order we recognize. For the sake of that order we risk our liberty, our good name. The time is past when good men can remain silent, when obedience can segregate men from public risk, when the poor can die without defense."

When an FBI agent arrived on the scene, he surveyed the raiders, and spotted Philip among them. "Good God," he reportedly said. "You again. I'm changing my religion."

Indeed, the act itself and the subsequent trial of the "Catonsville Nine," as they came to be known, was widely misunderstood and misinterpreted. The Berrigans landed on the cover of *Time* magazine, but the public was slow to sympathize and many saw the priests as renegades and madmen at best, traitors and terrorists at worst. Some among the anti-war movement did pick up the banner, however, and soon copy-cat raids on draft boards were reported around the country. In Milwaukee, a marauding band of peaceniks managed to destroy every last draft file in the entire city.

The Catonsville Nine's trial was quick and merciless. Daniel was sentenced to three years; Philip got three and a half, to run concurrent with the six-year sentence he had received for the earlier action in Baltimore. The other seven were also convicted of assault and destruction of government property and sentenced to various, mostly lesser, terms. None apologized for their actions, and on the stand, they each explained their personal and spiritual motivation. One of the nine, a Christian Brother named David Darst, testified, "You could say Jesus too was guilty of assault when he cast the money-changers out of the temple."

Though the trial was big news, the renegade priests were popularly seen more as cultural curiosities than moral patriots as they had hoped. If their statement hadn't been enough to get the country's attention, they would need to amplify it. "The media's addiction to violence is matched only by its contemptuous indifference to nonviolence," Daniel would later write in *To Dwell in Peace*.

"Blessed are you when they revile and persecute you, and say all kinds of evil against you falsely for My sake. Rejoice and be exceedingly glad, for great is your reward in heaven, for so they persecuted the prophets who were before you." —Matthew 5:11

Daniel Berrigan

MY COUNTRY, RIGHT OR WRONG?

The Catonsville action also brought the Berrigans into conflict with the Catholic Church, although the seeds of the conflict had been sown long before. Indeed, sometimes it's hard to tell whether Philip and Daniel Berrigan fought harder against war, or against the Catholic Church's complicit silence on the subject of war. The Church's ambivalence had bothered Daniel even in his earliest days as a Jesuit novice. His first theological questions arose during World War II. "Who indeed was this Christ? Who was He to us, our generation?" Daniel asked himself. "Who was He to technology and superpower politics and world wars...? Did Christ, to the point, if point there was, curse or rejoice in the carnage of war? And if He rejoiced, what of us? And if He cursed, what then?" he wondered.

He sought counsel from Thomas Merton through a correspondence spanning two decades. The two rolled the ideas over in their minds and hearts and traded insights on everything from Hiroshima to Vietnam. Still, he was torn between a contemplative, rhetorical approach, and hands-on involvement in the anti-war movement. In the late 1960s, Daniel began speaking out publicly against the war, and his superiors at first seemed not quite sure what to do with him.

They counseled him to tone down his rhetoric and stop endorsing anti-war demonstrations. When he refused, the Church exiled him to Central America. That turned out to be a huge mistake, attracting as it did accusations that the Church was trying to silence one of its own. Daniel came back a year later "worse than ever," and an overnight folk hero and revolutionary leader. His profile had been unintentionally heightened by the very institution that had wanted him to fade away. Daniel became a thorn in the side of the Church on the topic of war. "For a thousand years, the peacemaking Jesus had been out of fashion," he later wrote. "There remained only the assumption that cried to heaven for redress; instead of the declared criminality of all wars, Catholics were to assume the normalcy of war." It was as if Vietnam had once and for all turned off the critical and pacifist instincts of the Church itself. "The war signaled the end of the questioning of war," Daniel lamented.

UNDERGROUND

Daniel's exile also taught both brothers a crucial lesson: Sometimes the sheer fact of being punished—whether exiled by the Church or jailed by the government—accomplishes far more than the precipitating act of defiance or disobedience could. Their conviction for Catonsville would prove it for good. However, the Berrigans and their co-defendants decided after much thought to break with a key tenet of nonviolence: Some among them would refuse to pay the price for their actions.

"The system that sentenced me is the same foul system that is carrying on this war. I will defy it to the end. It does not deserve my allegiance," Daniel said.

Five of the nine, following their consciences and hoping to make an even bolder statement, failed to report to jail when their sentences were due to commence, and instead went underground. Philip would immortalize the new strategy by dubbing the group "fugitives from injustice." Quickly, FBI director J. Edgar Hoover—who was understandably irate at being shown up by what he saw as nothing more than a gaggle of peacenik nuns and priests—put the full weight of his agency behind capturing the fugitives. And sure enough, one by one, the fugitives were caught. All except Daniel Berrigan.

Daniel moved stealthily in the shadows for four months, staying with a series of friends and strangers and changing safe houses regularly. But he hardly disappeared. He toyed with Hoover by popping up at anti-war rallies and appearing in a nationally televised interview on network television. He gave his "Sermon from the Underground" in a Philadelphia church in front of a stunned congregation, then slipped away before FBI agents arrived. He attended an anti-war rally at Cornell that was crawling with FBI agents, and again slipped away, this time under a huge papier-mâché puppet of one of Christ's apostles. He was bold and daring and occasionally reckless, and he was also quite publicly thumbing his nose at the establishment responsible for the war. But his luck would run out soon enough.

The FBI paid a prison snitch to intercept a letter to Philip, which revealed plans to move Daniel to a friend's house on Block Island in Rhode Island. On a rainy day, the little house

A popular poster of this image asked "which of these men is free?"

Protest signs in the background read:

CTRINE
EMPTION
IRAQ

www.peacecoalition...

CH
FC
WA

DON
NVA
IRAQ

INVADE AMERICA

"Dan and I went to prison because we believe that Christianity and revolution are synonymous."
—Philip Berrigan

Daniel and Philip Berrigan in the 1990s

was surrounded by yellow-jacketed agents. Daniel gave himself up with a satisfied grin on his face. A photo of him being led away in handcuffs by two sour-faced officers, his head pitched back in a laugh, became a popular poster in 1970, bearing the legend "Which of these men is free?"

NEVER BACK DOWN

Daniel and Philip eventually served out their terms, but they never did fall silent. In 1973, they were nominated for the Nobel Peace Prize. Ironically, that year Henry Kissinger won for his "peace efforts" in Vietnam. Had the Berrigans won, however, they would not have been able to attend the ceremony anyway, since Philip was in prison again and Daniel was not allowed to leave the country as a condition of his parole. The brothers would again be nominated in 1998—this time by Irish laureate Mairead Maguire—but again they did not win.

Philip secretly married former nun Elizabeth McAlister and was excommunicated by the Catholic Church when the marriage was revealed. Together, the two of them founded Jonah House, a Catholic anti-war residential community dedicated to nonviolent protest, which was at one point characterized by the Baltimore probation department as a hotbed of "ongoing criminal activity." Many of its residents are elderly nuns and priests.

In 1980, Philip and Elizabeth also founded Plowshares, a loosely organized network of interfaith direct-action groups dedicated to opposing nuclear weapons and the U.S. military-industrial complex. Drawing directly from the Bible, the more than 70 Plowshares actions to date have been characterized by small groups of activists entering military installations, climbing onto weaponry such as missiles, submarines, warships, and airplanes, and pounding on them with hammers or spilling blood on the machinery of war. For this, hundreds of the activists have been arrested and served prison time for conspiracy, destruction of government property, criminal mischief, and a hodge-podge of other charges. In 2001 at age 78, Philip Berrigan—who had been characterized as a "terrorist" by half a dozen federal prosecutors and J. Edgar Hoover himself in the previous 30-odd years—marked a decade spent behind bars for his acts of civil disobedience. Philip died in Dec. 2002.

Daniel also continued writing and speaking out against war, even after Vietnam was over. His play *The Trial of the Catonsville Nine* became an anti-war classic, and has been translated into a half dozen languages and performed around the world. He traveled to Central America and protested U.S. involvement in destabilizing the region.

In the 1980s, he was active with Plowshares, and frequently seen at protests against the "Star Wars" missile defense system then proposed by the Reagan administration. He has spoken eloquently and controversially on Arab-Israeli tensions in the Middle East, and led multiple protests against U.S. involvement in Iraq, Kosovo, and Afghanistan. He still lives in a Jesuit community in Manhattan and is now 82 years old.

Daniel ruffled many of his liberal allies' feathers by emerging in the 1980s as a fervent anti-abortion activist. He and Philip have defended their pro-life philosophy as rooted in the same Biblical teaching that all life is sacred. They have contended, compellingly, that a faithful and "morally consistent" application of their ethic—that no principle is worth the cost of a human life—demands that they oppose war, capital punishment, and abortion in equal measure.

LEARN MORE

Jonah House/Plowshares
1301 Moreland Avenue
Baltimore
MD 21216
Tel: (410) 233-6238
Email: disarmnow@aol.com

The Berrigan-McAlister Collection
DePaul University Library
A collection of trial transcripts,
correspondence from prison, and
memorabilia associated with the
Berrigans' anti-Vietnam protests, the
founding of Jonah House, and a
chronology of Plowshares actions.

To Dwell in Peace: An Autobiography
by Daniel Berrigan
Harper and Row, 1987

**Disarmed and Dangerous: The Radical Lives
and Times of Daniel and Philip Berrigan**
by Murray Polner and Jim O'Grady
Plough Publishing House, 1997

**Fighting the Lamb's War: Skirmishes
with the American Empire**
by Philip Berrigan with Fred A. Wilcox
Common Courage Press, 1996

The Trial of the Catonsville Nine
by Daniel Berrigan
Beacon Press, 1970

Prison Journals of a Priest Revolutionary
by Philip Berrigan with Vincent McGee
Holt, Rinehart and Winston, 1970

Trial Poems
by Daniel Berrigan
Beacon Press, 1970

**Steadfastness of the Saints: A Journal of
Peace and War in Central and North America**
by Daniel Berrigan
Maryknoll, N.Y., 1985

"I HAD NO RIGHT"

(FROM *THE GREEN WORLD*) BY DAR WILLIAMS

God of the poor man, this is how the day began
Eight codefendants, I, Daniel Berrigan
Oh, and only a layman's batch of Napalm
We pulled the draft files out
We burned them in the parking lot
Better the files than the bodies of children

I had no right but for the love of you
I had no right but for the love of you

Many roads led here, walked with the suffering
Tom in Guatemala, Philip in New Orleans
Oh it's a long road from law to justice
I went to Vietnam, I went for peace
They dropped their bombs
Right where my government knew I would be

I had no right but for the love of you

And all my country saw
Were priests who broke the law

First it was a question, then it was a mission
How to be American, how to be a Christian
Oh, if their law is their cross and the cross is burning

I had no right but for the love of you

God of the just, I'll never win a peace prize
Falling like Jesus
Now let the jury rise
Oh it's all of us versus all that paper
They took the only way they know who is on trial today
Deliver us unto each other, I pray

I had no right but for the love of you
And every trial I stood, I stood for you

Eyes on the trial
8 a.m. arrival
Hands on the Bible

(Dar Williams sang "I Had No Right" at
a private concert at the United States
Supreme Court in April 2002)

TRIDENT PLOUGHSHARES

BRITISH INTERFAITH PEACE ACTIVISTS

The European outgrowth of the Berrigans' Plowshares action network, Trident Ploughshares is an interfaith organization headquartered in the United Kingdom, dedicated to nuclear disarmament. The U.K.'s Trident nuclear weapons system centers on four submarines based near Glasgow, Scotland. Each submarine carries up to 16 Trident missiles, and each missile carries several 100-kiloton warheads. The British government acquires Trident weapons from U.S. military contractors.

Like Plowshares in the United States, Trident Ploughshares activists enact the Biblical injunction to "beat swords into ploughshares" by climbing onto airplanes, submarines, and other war machines and either damaging them with hammers or carefully dismantling them. While it began as a Christian movement, it now embraces members from disparate spiritual backgrounds.

The group's mission statement says, "The underlying appeal is the universal call to peace, to abolish all war and to find peaceful ways to resolve our conflicts. It recognizes the abuse of power that war always is, and the deep immorality of threats to kill." In 1995, four women did extensive damage to a British Aerospace Hawk jet in a Ploughshares action. The plane had been scheduled to be exported to Indonesia, where the government was using such weaponry against the civilian population of East Timor. The plane was never shipped. The women were

ACT NOW www.tridentploughshares.org

" Blessed are the peacemakers, for they will be called sons of God."
—Matthew 5:9

ON THIS DAY IN 1945. A CITY OF 250,000 PEOPLE WAS DESTROYED BY AN ATOM BOMB. HIROSHIMA WE REMEMBER DO YOU?

STOP TRIDENT

acquitted after successfully arguing that their act was legally justified because they were preventing British complicity in genocide.

In 1998, Ploughshares protesters commandeered a police boat from within the high-security perimeter at a Trident base near Glasgow. In 40 minutes, they took it through the lochs and into another high-security area, where they landed a woman only yards away from two Trident submarines.

One of the protestors, Angie Zelter, said, "We were putting it to its right and proper use—taxpayers expect police equipment to be used to uphold the law. That is what we did, we used the boat to investigate the ongoing British conspiracy to commit war crimes and grave breaches of international humanitarian law with weapons of mass destruction."

As of April 2000, Ploughshares activists had been subject to more than 1,700 arrests, almost 300 trials, over 1,600 days in prison, and more than £41,000 in fines and penalties.

❤ GET INVOLVED

Trident Ploughshares
42-46 Bethel St., Norwich
Norfolk, NR2 1NR
Email: info@tridentploughshares.org
Tel: 0845 45 88 366 or ++441259 753815
Web site: www.tridentploughshares.org

DOROTHY DAY

FOUNDER, CATHOLIC WORKER MOVEMENT

Dorothy Day—often called the "saint of the homeless"—was a friend, colleague, and inspiration to the Berrigan brothers. Founder of the Catholic Worker Movement, she was already an icon in the American religious left when the Berrigans were in diapers.

Day was a journalist with a special interest in the problem of poverty, and came to pacifism and Catholicism rather late in life after an out-of-wedlock pregnancy. In 1933, after struggling for years to reconcile her newfound faith with her social conscience, she founded the Catholic Worker Movement with Peter Maurin, and together they grew their simple concept of voluntary poverty and service to the poor into a thriving international community and movement.

She and her followers lived lives of voluntary poverty among the homeless and desperate in America's inner cities, Day primarily in Chicago. Catholic Worker Houses are scattered in urban centers across America, dedicated to providing shelter and food to the needy.

Dorothy Day Centers, like this one in St. Paul, Minnesota, provide food and shelter to the needy.

During Vietnam, Day openly opposed the war and adopted a personal ethic of pacifism. She also championed the causes of civil rights and organized labor, supporting and befriending leaders from Martin Luther King Jr. to Cesar Chavez. Day wrote several books, including an autobiography entitled *The Long Loneliness* (Harper & Brothers, 1952). Filmmaker Father Bud Kaiser, who in 1996 made *Entertaining Angels: The Dorothy Day Story*, calls Day "a feisty, street-smart, yet compassionate American Mother Teresa—but a Mother Teresa with a past!"

❤ GET INVOLVED

The following are Christian or ecumenical organizations concerned with peace and justice issues.

Catholic Worker
www.catholicworker.com

PaxChristi USA
www.paxchristiusa.org

Plowshares Actions
www.plowsharesactions.org

Nonviolence Web
www.nonviolence.org

United For Peace
www.unitedforpeace.org

Peace Action
www.peace-action.org

Witness for Peace
www.witnessforpeace.org

Fellowship of Reconciliation
www.forusa.org

Ecumenical Peace Institute
www.epicalc.org

Project Plowshares, Canada
www.ploughshares.ca

World Council of Churches
www.wcc-coe.org

Catholic Peace Fellowship
www.catholicpeacefellowship.org

International Committee for the Peace Council
www.peacecouncil.org

DIVINE

OBEDIENCE

FATHER ROY BOURGEOIS

CATHOLIC PRIEST, FOUNDER OF
SCHOOL OF THE AMERICAS WATCH

He looked every bit the part: a distinguished middle-aged man with a Southern drawl, nattily dressed in a colonel's uniform. You really can't blame the guards at the US Army's Fort Benning, near Columbus, Georgia, for waving him and his cohorts through the heavy gates that evening in 1983. They must have looked like any other officers out for their evening constitutional.

Once inside the gates, the colonel headed for a stand of trees near the barracks where two dozen Salvadoran soldiers were just turning in after a hard day's combat training. The colonel clambered up a pine tree with a boom-box strapped to his back. He held the radio above his head and shouted "Bishop Romero, this is for you, brother!" and hit *Play*. The air was filled with Archbishop Oscar Romero's last homily, delivered the night before he was assassinated by a government-controlled death squad in El Salvador: "This is an appeal to those in the barracks. Stop the killing! Lay down your arms! Disobey your superiors who are telling you to kill! Stop the oppression! Stop the oppression!"

Romero had been dead three years by the time his words rang out of that Southern pine forest and into the ears of soldiers who were visibly shaken by them. And as Roy Bourgeois, the mischief maker in the trees, was yanked down, roughed up, handcuffed, and turned over

"You begin to speak,
you begin to break
your silence.

And that is sacred in
that it brings us
deeper into the struggle."

—Fr. Roy Bourgeois

to police and FBI agents, he knew he had found his true calling.

Although he is a former Navy lieutenant with a Purple Heart from a tour in Vietnam, Roy Bourgeois is neither colonel nor warrior. That Army uniform was borrowed; Father Roy usually wears the white collar of his current profession. A Catholic Maryknoll priest, he has dedicated his life to shutting down the School of the Americas, a U.S. Army–run training center for Latin American military officers that has taught 60,000 soldiers the finer points of torture, assassination, and oppression. And his prank that night in 1983 was a precursor to a storied career in dramatic, soulful, highly targeted, nonviolent civil disobedience.

Roy Bourgeois, a small-town Louisiana Cajun boy who grew up splitting time between school, church, and various sports, could not have had a more down-home, all-American, patriotic beginning. He joined the Navy after college, and volunteered for a tour of shore duty in Vietnam. He had been asked to do his part to kill godless Communists and "liberate" a country he had barely heard of, and he went with enthusiasm.

While there, he spent almost all of his free time sneaking into the jungle to help out at a tiny, run-down orphanage set up by a Catholic missionary there. The hut housed 300 children whose parents—some of them "godless Communists"—had been killed in the war. Bourgeois saw combat; he witnessed several of his friends killed by Viet Cong, and was himself wounded and nearly killed in a bombing raid. He was sent home to a hero's welcome in Lutcher, Louisiana. But Bourgeois was a changed man. He had become a man of peace, not of war.

"I learned something very important, that this was something very sacred when one reaches that moment or that point on the journey where your faith brings you to giving out a leaflet, brings you to the picket line, where you can begin to make decisions for yourself," Bourgeois said to *Loaves & Fishes* magazine in 1999. "You begin to speak, you begin to break your silence. And that is sacred in that it brings us deeper into the struggle."

In 1968, he was accepted into a seminary of the Maryknoll Missionary order, which is dedicated to working with the poor and oppressed in Third World countries.
By 1972, he was an ordained Catholic priest assigned to work with the poor in Bolivia. He was largely unaware that the desperation, poverty, and exploitation of the Bolivian people was common throughout Latin America at the time.

During the five years he lived, worked, ministered to the poor in La Paz, Father Roy helped set up a human-rights commission with local miners, students, and factory workers, and began to speak out about government-sponsored oppression of the Bolivian people. He felt that's what he'd been sent there to do. Not surprisingly, the Bolivian government—in particular Bolivian dictator General Hugo Banzar—was not amused by this naïve priest, and had him arrested and deported. By the time he was ejected from Bolivia, Father Roy was becoming aware of Liberation Theology's growing influence in Latin America, and the work being done by other missionaries in other poverty stricken dictatorships in the region.

In 1980, news reached him of the brutal assassination of Archbishop Romero, who was gunned down by a Salvadoran death squad as he said Mass. Romero had taken up the cause of land rights in El Salvador and provoked the ire of the government by speaking out against its militant oppression of the poor and landless.

Nine months after Romero's assassination, four Catholic nuns, two of them friends of Bourgeois, were raped and murdered by the same death squads. Several months later, those death squads wiped out the entire village of El Mozote—900 men, women, and children—in an attempt to scare future missionaries and insurgents. Father Roy, like many clergy at the time, was shattered, but also inspired.

"We began as priests and nuns connecting to the martyrdom of the priests and nuns of El Salvador," he said years later. "We soon realized through our research that not only were Church leaders being killed, but all those working in defense of the poor, including labor leaders, health-care workers, and those calling for land reform."

Father Roy did some digging and discovered that Roberto D'Aubuisson, the chief of El Salvador's death squads, had been trained by the U.S. Army at the School of the Americas (SOA).

DICTATOR - HUGO BANZAR
TRAINED BY AMERICA

MANUEL NORIEGA
DICTATOR
TRAINED BY AMERICA

GRADUATES OF THE
SCHOOL OF THE AMERICAS

ROBERTO D'AUBUISSON
HEAD OF DEATH SQUADS
TRAINED BY AMERICA

MEMBERS OF
PINOCHET'S SECRET POLICE
TRAINED BY AMERICA

El Chacal

Presented

to.....

Date.....

A little more digging, and he learned that General Banzar, the Bolivian dictator who had had him arrested and deported three years prior for advocating for human rights, was also a graduate of SOA. Other graduates, he subsequently discovered, included Panama's Manuel Noriega, several officers in charge of Chile's secret police under dictator Augusto Pinochet, and dozens more of the cruelest, most murderous men in Central and South America.

Enraged, Father Roy mounted his first covert invasion of the school—the boom-box serenade in 1983. He was sentenced to 18 months in prison on charges of trespass, impersonating an officer, and assault by Judge Robert "Maximum Bob" Elliott—the Southern segregationist judge who had also sent Martin Luther King Jr. to jail for civil disobedience, and who had acquitted the U.S. Army officer responsible for the My Lai massacre in Vietnam. Both Father Roy and Judge Elliott were just getting started; over the next 20 years Father Roy would mount dozens of protests at Fort Benning, and Maximum Bob would sentence him on several more occasions for a total of more than four years in federal prison.

Then, in 1989, six Jesuit priests, their housekeeper, and her 15-year-old daughter were brutally massacred in El Salvador by D'Aubuisson's death squads. Father Roy pledged to do to whatever it took, for however long it took, and with whatever sacrifice, to shut down the school, which he has renamed the "School of Assassins."

In 1990, he founded School of the Americas Watch (SOAW), and moved into a tiny apartment just outside Ft. Benning's gates. He organized a protest at the school, something to rival his boom-box coup, in honor of his fallen brothers. On the first anniversary of the massacre, Father Roy, his friend Rev. Charles Liteky, and Charles' brother Patrick, had a nurse draw pints

> *"They tell me I am breaking the law by trespassing, but I follow a higher law. A law that says suffering must be stopped."*—**Fr. Roy Bourgeois**

of their own blood and place it into plastic containers. The three men walked onto the Army base in broad daylight, and into its "Hall of Fame" building, where distinguished graduates are celebrated. They splashed the vials of their blood on the walls, and left a letter to the commandant calling for the closure of the SOA. They also left gruesome photographs of the massacre. Then they lay down in pools of their own blood and waited to be arrested. They served 14 months in federal prison for the action.

Father Roy has now spent five of his 64 years in federal prison for the nonviolent protest he organizes every year at Fort Benning. His crime in most of the cases is trespassing. He marches onto the military base, reenacts the murders, then leads a somber funeral procession. For this, he has been arrested and sentenced to federal prison over and over again.

Each year, he's joined by more of SOA Watch's supporters—now more than 12,000 people participate. At the 2001 protest, 43 people were arrested for trespassing, and all who were "repeat offenders" were sentenced to 3 to 6 months in federal prison and up to $1,000 in fines. Many of those arrested and convicted each year are priests and nuns, most of them over 60 years old, and many with missionary experience in places where the civilian population is terrorized by SOA graduates.

SOA: SCHOOL OF ASSASSINS

73 percent of those cited for human rights abuses in 1980s

✝✝✝✝✝✝✝✝✝✝✝✝✝✝✝✝✝✝✝✝✝✝✝✝✝✝

2 of the 3 men who gunned down Archbishop Romero

19 of the 26 men who massacred six Jesuit priests

🔫🔫🔫🔫🔫🔫🔫🔫🔫🔫🔫🔫🔫🔫🔫🔫🔫🔫🔫🔫🔫🔫🔫🔫🔫🔫

10 of the 12 officers responsible for the civilian massacre at El Mozote

⊕⊕⊕⊕⊕⊕⊕⊕⊕⊕⊕⊕

source: 1993 UN Truth Commission Report

Father Roy has proven himself time and again to be on the side of the angels. In the early 1990s SOA Watch provoked a United Nations investigation of the SOA's actions in El Salvador. In 1993, the UN Truth Commission released a report on El Salvador that revealed that 73 percent of El Salvadorans cited for human-rights abuses in the 1980s were graduates of the SOA: 2 of the 3 men who gunned down Archbishop Romero; 19 of the 26 men who massacred the Jesuit priests and their 2 civilian friends; 10 of the 12 officers responsible for the civilian massacre at El Mozote...and the list goes on.

Later it was revealed that instructors were using CIA manuals endorsing torture, illegal arrest and detention, and psychological manipulation to control "enemies of the state"—all of which the school had vehemently denied. Father Roy notes that the "enemies" and "insurgents" in almost all of these cases are nothing but the poor and the desperate who decide to stand up for themselves against corrupt and abusive dictatorships.

In a recent video from SOA Watch called *SOA: Guns, Greed, and Globalization*, Father Roy calls the SOA little more than the military arm of the International Monetary Fund and World Bank. It protects the wealthy elite in Latin America and preserves the ability of multinational corporations to exploit cheap labor and resources there.

In 2000, the U.S. Congress changed the name of the school to the Western Hemisphere Institute for Security Cooperation, and promised to institute new courses in human rights and democratic processes. Father Roy says this is just cynical window dressing, and that the dirty old business of milling career despots continues inside the shiny new exterior. Today Father Roy is still fighting to close the school, and finds that the U.S. "War on Terrorism" is exactly the right reason to keep fighting. "Why not start right here on U.S. soil?" he asks. Indeed, he says President George W. Bush and his administration are the worst kind of hypocrites: Al-Qaeda recruits men from other countries, transports them to highly secretive training camps, inculcates them in a very specific ideology about how the world and its nations should be run, trains them in brutality, and then ships them off to commit acts of horror upon innocent people thousands of miles away. Which is precisely, says Father Roy, what the U.S. government does at the School of the Americas.

LEARN MORE

SOA Watch
PO Box 4566
Washington, DC 20017
Tel.: 202-234-3440
Fax: 202-636-4505
Email: info@soaw.org
Web site: www.soaw.org

BOOKS

Solidarity in Action: A Guide for Grassroots Organizing to Close the SOA
School of the Americas Watch, 2001

Prophets Without Honor: A Requiem for Moral Patriotism
by William Strabala, Michael Palecek
Algora Publishing, 2002

School of Assassins
by Jack Nelson-Pallmeyer,
with introduction by Father Roy Bourgeois
Orbis Books, 2001

VIDEOS
(All available through SOA Watch and at some bookstores.)

**Father Roy: Inside the School of Assassins
School of Assassins
SOA: Guns, Greed, and Globalization
The New Patriots
Crossing the Line**

EVIL OF THE SOA

(to the tune of "Battle of Jericho")

We all shook the evil of the SOA, the SOA, the SOA
We all shook the evil of the SOA —and the walls came a tumbling down.

You can talk about training soldiers
You can talk about human rights
But we all know the truth about the SOA
And the walls will come a tumblin' down.

Many spirits walk before us
Their witness makes the sound
Of a heartbeat fueled by fire
And the walls come a tumblin' down.

We gathered at Ft. Benning
Twelve thousand people strong
'Cause the truth will not be silenced,
As we lift our voices in song.

Well, I've heard God's voice on the mountaintop
In the desert and by the sea
Crying, "Rise up against those SOA walls
And you too shall be free!"

SONGS FROM THE FT. BENNING PROTESTS

DOROTHY HENNESSEY

CATHOLIC NUN, SOA WATCH ACTIVIST

Dorothy Hennessey is an 89-year-old nun with the Sisters of Saint Francis of the Holy Family. She lives in a retirement home for nuns in Dubuque, Iowa, now, but in her younger years she served as a missionary in Central America. She was an observer at the 1990 Nicaraguan elections.

Sister Dorothy attended the School of the Americas Watch protest in November 2000, and was arrested for trespassing on U.S. military property. When the judge offered to sentence her to 6 months under house arrest instead of federal prison, she refused, saying she wanted to receive the same punishment as her two dozen co-defendants.

Her sister Gwen, 68, is also a Franciscan nun in Dubuque, and was also arrested for trespassing and sentenced to 6 months in prison. They were both released in January 2002.

ACT NOW   www.soaw.org

CLOSE THE
SCHOOL OF THE AMERICAS!

(STAND UP FOR JUSTICE)

(to the tune of "Wade in the Water")

Chorus:
Stand up for justice! Stand up for justice, people!
Stand up for justice! Close the School of the Americas!

It's a school of assassins, a school of shame!
(Close the School of the Americas!)

Not with my money, and not in my name!
(Close the School of the Americas!)

They killed Oscar Romero in El Salvador!
Close the School of the Americas!)

They're waging a war against the poor!
(Close the School of the Americas!)

They teach torture, murder, hatred, and fear!
(Close the School of the Americas!)

Too many dead, too many disappeared!
(Close the School of the Americas!)

MARTIN SHEEN

CATHOLIC ACTOR AND ACTIVIST

Martin Sheen, better known these days as Catholic president Jeb Bartlett on TV's *West Wing*, was born Ramon Estevez. He changed his name to avoid rampant racism in Hollywood, and adopted his new surname from a Catholic 1950s television evangelist, Bishop Fulton Sheen, whom he admired.

He has counted himself a friend of Cesar Chavez, Daniel Berrigan, Roy Bourgeois, and numerous other prominent labor and anti-war activists, and has been arrested in nonviolent protests alongside almost all of them.

Sheen regularly protests nuclear weapons testing in the Nevada desert with the interfaith group The Nevada Desert Experience. He has been arrested for civil disobedience associated with a strawberry worker's strike, and has marched against United States plans for missile defense systems (Sheen's first arrest for protesting was at such a rally in 1997, with Daniel Berrigan).

ACT NOW   www.nevadadesertexperience.org

Ralph Nader even approached Sheen to be his running mate on the Green Party ticket in 1996, but Sheen politely declined, saying he wasn't intelligent enough to be in the White House. In the film of Dorothy Day's life, *Entertaining Angels*, Sheen played Peter Maurin. The French laborer and former Christian Brother was Dorothy Day's mentor and co-founder of the Catholic Worker Movement.

❤️ LEARN MORE

Nevada Desert Experience
An ecumenical group that has gathered each Lent since 1982 at the United States Nevada Test Site to protest nuclear weapons proliferation.
PO Box 46645, Las Vegas, NV 89114-6645
Tel.: (702) 646 4814
Email: nde@peacenet.org
Web site: www.nevadadesertexperience.org

Shundahai Network
An indigenous-ecumenical partnership in Southern Nevada and Utah dedicated to nuclear disarmament, Shundahai means "peace and harmony with all creation" in Newe, a Western Shoshone language.
1350 E. Flamingo Box 255, Las Vegas, NV 89119
Tel.: 702.369.2730
Email: kalynda@shundahai.org
Web site: www.shundahai.org

OSCAR ARNULFO ROMERO

ARCHBISHOP OF EL SALVADOR

Oscar Romero died as he had lived: ministering to the poor and defending the defenseless. He was gunned down as he said Mass at the altar of the Church of the Divine Providence by an ultra-rightist death squad aligned with the El Salvadoran government.

As Archbishop of El Salvador in the tumultuous 1970s, he began as a quiet, conservative, uncontroversial head of the Catholic Church in San Salvador. But as he became increasingly aware of the suffering of the poorest among his congregation, he began to question the military juntas which effectively ran his country at the time.

He sent an open letter to *The New York Times* just a few weeks before his murder, pleading with then-President Jimmy Carter to cut off military aid to El Salvador. Just a day before his assassination, he called on El Salvador's soldiers—many of them conscripted against their will and ordered to murder their innocent neighbors—to lay down their weapons and work for peace.

Among his last words to his congregation: "We know that every effort to better society, especially when injustice and sin are so ingrained, is an effort that God blesses, that God wants, that God demands of us."

ACT NOW   www.rtfcam.org

Este pueblo aprendera a sonreir, ser verdaderamente alegre, cuando se realice una verdadera transformación." (Mons. Romero)

oikos Solidaridad

Hacia la Gestión Sustentable del Agua en El Salva...

The United States CIA has recently been implicated in Romero's murder. The CIA was covertly helping the groups in power put down what it saw as potential "Communist insurgencies," and Romero had been openly advocating military mutiny and a peasant uprising.

Mourners in El Salvador mark the anniversary of Archbishop Romero's death.

❤ LEARN MORE

The Religious Task Force on Central America and Mexico
The RTFCAM was founded by Catholic religious leaders in March 1980 in response to Archbishop Romero's call for international solidarity with the people of El Salvador.

3053 Fourth St. NE
Washington, DC 20017
Tel.: (202) 529-0441
Email: sfinke@rtfcam.org
Web site: www.rtfcam.org

GET INVOLVED

The following organizations, most of them pacifist interfaith groups, are dedicated to peace and justice issues in Latin America.

Fellowship of Reconciliation – Task Force on Latin America and the Caribbean

Part of The Fellowship of Reconciliation (FOR), a national, interfaith, pacifist organization in the United States, the Task Force helps nonviolent peace organizations work together to affect change in the region.
www.forusa.org/Programs/TFLAC.html

Latin America Working Group

The Latin America Working Group (LAWG) is a coalition of more than 60 religious, human rights, policy, grassroots and development organizations.
www.lawg.org

Witness for Peace

A grassroots group working for peace, social and economic justice, and human rights in Latin America.
www.witnessforpeace.org

Office of the Americas

Founded by Blasé Bonpane, the Office of the Americas is dedicated to the peaceful opposition to U.S. military policy in Latin America.
www.officeoftheamericas.org

Pax Christi USA

The focal organizing point of the Catholic peace movement in the United States
www.paxchristiusa.org

Resource Center of the Americas

Not a religious group, the Resource Center is focused primarily on preventing and ameliorating the negative effects of globalization on Latin America and Latin Americans.
http://americas.org

Peace Brigades

Peace Brigades International (PBI) is a non-governmental organization that protects human rights and promotes nonviolent transformation of conflicts.
www.peacebrigades.org

THE RADICAL

HUMANIST

JOHN TRUDELL

SANTEE SIOUX INDIGENOUS RIGHTS ACTIVIST

On February 11, 1979, John Trudell strode up the steps of the J. Edgar Hoover Building in Washington D.C., with a speech in his head and an American flag in his hand. He may have known that inside the building at that moment, his own full-to-bursting file held more than 17,000 pages of data, rumors, and outright fabrications. The FBI hated Trudell—and the feeling was mutual

As the afternoon began to wane, Trudell addressed the crowd of several hundred Native Americans and supporters who had marched there from the Supreme Court, demanding justice for Leonard Peltier. All assembled believed that Peltier, who was on death row, had been framed for the murders of two FBI agents on the Pine Ridge Reservation in 1975.

As he stood before the crowd, Trudell—a Santee Sioux from Nebraska who had been National Chairman of the American Indian Movement (AIM) for 6 of its most controversial years—decried the long history of the U.S. government's persecution of Native Americans. He delivered a scathing indictment of the FBI's covert war on AIM, which had culminated a few years before with the second massacre at Wounded Knee and with the Peltier incident. Trudell railed against the FBI's CoIntelPro (domestic counterintelligence programs), which targeted political movements such as the Black Panthers and AIM, and used agents-provocateur, spurious arrests, and harassment to bring the nascent radical movements to their knees.

 ACT NOW   www.johntrudell.com

"My grandparents didn't teach me spirituality, they taught me wisdom. There's a difference."
—John Trudell

By the end of Trudell's speech that cold February day, the thronging crowd pulsed with anger.

And then, declaring that it had been desecrated by the government's own racism, deceit, and economic thuggery, Trudell held the flag upside down, pulled out a Zippo and set it alight. It would be Trudell's last public act of defiance as chairman of AIM. A few hours later, 2,000 miles away, Trudell's wife, mother-in-law, and three small children would die in a suspicious fire on the Duck Valley Shoshone Paiute reservation in Nevada. Trudell believes the FBI, the CIA, and the Bureau of Indian Affairs (BIA) conspired to set the blaze in order murder his family and shut him up.

He had been warned, after all. While in the Springfield Federal Prison Hospital in 1978, a fellow inmate—a man he had never met before—cautioned Trudell to tone down his rhetoric or stop his activism altogether, or his family would be in danger. The inmate never revealed the source of his information, but Trudell knew that the federal government had had him in

its sights for years and would stop at nothing to crush AIM. But he could not, in good conscience, give up or allow himself to be intimidated into silence. He says today that he does not regret staying with AIM as long as he did, but he also could not go on after the fire. About a month after the tragedy, he left AIM for good.

The house fire was eventually ruled an accident by the BIA, and the FBI refused to investigate, despite copious evidence of arson. "It was murder," Trudell says now. "They were murdered as an act of war." By that horrible day, Trudell was a veteran of that war, the war between the federal government and a new generation of Native activists.

RELUCTANT WARRIOR

Trudell was born February 15, 1946, on the Santee Sioux reservation near Omaha, Nebraska. His father was Santee, his mother of Mexican native descent. Trudell's mother died when he was only 6, and his father struggled to care for John and his siblings. For the next 11 years, John was shuttled between his father and his grandparents, always struggling to get enough to eat. Although he spent about half of his childhood on the reservation, he says didn't feel fully connected to the traditions and spiritual myths of his culture at that time.

"My grandparents didn't teach me spirituality, they taught me wisdom. There's a difference," Trudell says in his usual blunt, unapologetic way. "The stories they told me were basically just lessons, although they may have been couched in different language. But the messages were simple: Do the right thing. Do the best you can with what you have. Respect life. We didn't consider that religion, we considered it reality."

The tough times of his childhood, the scarcity, and the racism he encountered from whites in the community were early ingredients of his later radicalism. After a few years of wandering, dropping out of college and drifting from job to job, in 1963 he joined the military. His decision didn't spring from any particular allegiance to his country or attraction to war—the military was the one way he could see out of the poverty surrounding him. Knowing that as a poor minority he would be a prime candidate for infantry in the Army or Marines, he entered the Navy, to "minimize my chances of becoming a rifle-toting target."

After a tour of duty in Vietnam, Trudell returned and resumed seeking a path for his life. He tried college again, but it just didn't seem to suit him. And then, in 1969, he read about something happening in San Francisco that piqued his interest. A group of Native Americans calling themselves "Indians of All Tribes" had landed on Alcatraz Island, site of an infamous decommissioned federal prison, and claimed it as "Indian Land." Trudell found himself drawn to the place. The minute he set foot on the rocky outcropping a mile offshore in the San Francisco Bay, "I knew this was for me."

Suddenly, he felt reconnected with his tribal roots. Something about the political struggle appealed to him, and many around him watched as this stranger blossomed into a natural leader. Within weeks, Trudell was the official spokesman of the occupying Indians.

For almost two years, the Indians held the island, living in former warden and guards' quarters and ferrying provisions in from sympathizers on shore. Trudell expertly handled the media, and turned a local news curiosity into a national news sensation. Soon the occupation was in every newspaper and on every nightly newscast.

The occupation, which ended in 1971 when federal agents reclaimed the island, would go down in the history books as the first major salvo in the new Native American rights movement. Trudell, suddenly thrust into the spotlight and proving his mettle, joined the leadership of AIM, which included Russell Banks and Dennis Means.

THE AIM YEARS

In the early 1970s, AIM was riding high on huge public and reservation support. The group organized several more high-profile occupations including a sit-in at Mount Rushmore in 1971 and a two-day take-over of the BIA headquarters in Washington, D.C., in 1972. The occupation of the BIA building made international news, thanks largely to Trudell's skill as a reasonable and eloquent spokesman.

The Nixon administration was humiliated by the publicity, especially since the occupation occurred the week of Congressional elections. In the end, AIM agreed to decamp on the condition that none of the occupiers be prosecuted, and with the Nixon administration's promise to prepare a careful response to AIM's "Twenty Points," a list of demands for changing the federal government's relationship with the Indian nations. But the BIA occupation left the federal government embittered and hungry for revenge.

Trudell returned to his home on the Duck Valley reservation in Nevada, and was working on a scathing report detailing theft of federal money intended for Native American youth. AIM had uncovered evidence that the Bureau of Indian Affairs was ostensibly providing funding for reservation schools, but that many states were pocketing the money or dumping it into a general school fund, leaving nothing for kids on the reservations. But while Trudell toiled,

ACT NOW   www.johntrudell.com

passions were boiling over between his fellow activists and the federal government. Trudell knew that a confrontation—perhaps even a bloody one—was imminent. But he chose to stay in Nevada with his new wife, who was pregnant with their first child. He was kept informed of developments through the AIM grapevine.

According to official documents unearthed in the late 1970s, after the BIA occupation the federal government quickly mapped out a strategy to eliminate AIM. The plan involved co-opting the corruptible tribal leadership on the Pine Ridge reservation by paying off Oglala Sioux tribal president Dickie Wilson. The BIA gave Wilson, a power-hungry and vain man, a $64,000 grant to create a "tribal ranger group" (dubbed the Guardians of the Oglala Nation, or the "GOON squads"). The BIA and FBI endowed the squads with undercover agents, and together they declared open season on members of AIM.

By March of 1973, the atmosphere was ripe for confrontation. After several attempts by AIM to seek redress of their complaints, any hope of negotiation crumbled as the BIA, FBI, and Wilson's GOONs closed ranks. Federal troops appeared on the reservation, further antagonizing AIM. More than 100 AIM supporters gathered in a church in the reservation town of Wounded Knee, site of the 1890 massacre of Sioux by U.S. Cavalry and homesteader vigilantes. The location would prove all too apt.

After more than a month of tense negotiations, a firefight broke out. Over the next 10 days, two AIM members were killed, 14 wounded, and as many as 12 disappeared, never to be seen again. Over the next three years, the FBI's war on AIM reached a fever pitch. According to documents obtained through the Freedom of Information Act, the FBI and BIA used

"We must not become confused and deceived by their illusions. There is no such thing as military power; there is only military terrorism. There is no such thing as economic power; there is only economic exploitation. That is all that it is. They try to program our minds and fool us with these illusions so that we will believe that they hold the power in their hands but they do not."

—John Trudell
in his book Stickman

counterinsurgency tactics—including spying and infiltration—to divide and conquer AIM. According to Ward Churchill and Jim Vander Wall in their seminal book *The COINTELPRO Papers: Documents from the FBI's Secret Wars Against Dissent in the United States* (South End Press, 1990), between 1973 and 1976, more than 60 AIM members died violently near Pine Ridge, and most of those deaths were never investigated or prosecuted.

Trudell, known as a level-headed, thoughtful leader, had been appointed National Chairman of AIM shortly after Wounded Knee to lead the movement through these most troubled times. But his high profile at Alcatraz and the BIA occupation had already caught and kept the attention of the FBI. His FBI file, obtained in 1986 under the Freedom of Information Act, reads in part:

> "Trudell is an intelligent individual and eloquent speaker who has the ability to stimulate people into action. Trudell is a known hardliner who openly advocates and encourages the use of violence [i.e., armed self-defense] although he himself never becomes involved in the fighting.... Trudell has the ability to meet with a group of pacifists and in a short time have them yelling and screaming 'right-on!' In short, he is an extremely effective agitator."

But by 1979, both the FBI and the violence Trudell had personally avoided at Wounded Knee, had finally caught up with him. A month after the fire that killed his family, he stepped down as chairman and left AIM for good.

"I left AIM in 1979 because I was just done," he says. "That part of my life was finished. My leaving AIM was inevitable even before the fire, it was just a matter of when. But after the fire

I just didn't have the energy. Reality had changed for me. I could not go back to their reality and I couldn't bring them into my new reality. I had been exiled from their reality and there was no way I could go back. It was just so devastating that I knew I could never be in the same reality as them ever again."

In a sense, AIM was finished when Trudell left. Fragments of it remain today, but its strength was sapped and its allegiances shattered by years of FBI undermining. These days, various factions claim to be the true AIM, but none has the political savvy or effectiveness the group had under Trudell. Trudell, however, has no regrets. "Reality changes and you better change with it, or you lose. Ask the dinosaurs. I had a responsibility to those who were murdered. I had to survive what had been done, I had to find a way to endure."

Trudell's survival took the shape of poetry. He began writing in the months after his family's murder, and in the past 30 years he has become a prominent poet, musician, and actor. He has worked extensively with Jackson Browne, and Bob Dylan called his 1992 album, *AKA Graffiti Man*, the "best album of the year." His creations are filled with Native American imagery and iconography, as well as a healthy dose of still-fresh rage. "I was speaking at some conference a couple years ago, and a guy came up to me and told me that I was spiritually disconnected because I have so much anger," Trudell says. "And I told him, 'Maybe you're the one who's disconnected because you *don't*.'"

Despite the rich spiritual tradition of Trudell's own culture, he does not consider himself a spiritual leader in any conventional sense, and he has deep suspicions of people who call him, or themselves for that matter, "spiritual." "I never considered myself a spiritual leader. I

ACT NOW   www.johntrudell.com

just figured I had a spirit, and it was my attitude. A bad attitude," he laughs. "It is not my objective to be a leader, to get people to follow me. I don't like people behind me. But if something I say or do makes someone think—even if I don't change their mind—I've done my job."

His approach to faith is unconventional. Ask him what he believes in, and he'll tell you flat out: "Nothing. There are things I either know, or don't know. Everything else I choose to think about. I think the world needs less believing and more thinking." He says Native American "beliefs" are not really beliefs at all, but "ancestral knowledge."

"We are a spirit, we are a natural part of the earth, and all of our ancestors, all of our relations who have gone to the spirit world, they are here with us. That's power. They will help us. They will help us to see if we are willing to look. We are not separated from them because there's no place to go —
we stay here.

This is our place: the earth. This is our mother: we will not go away from our mother." —John Trudell

Trudell marks his skepticism of mystical metaphor from grade-school, when a teacher recounted the story of Pandora's Box. "The gods gave Pandora a box and told her not to open it because it contained the Seven Evils of the world. Of course, she opened the box. And out came the Seven Evils. But then Hope came out of the box, to help us deal with the evils. I always questioned that. The eighth thing to come out of that box was Hope. Hope was the eighth evil of the world, then, right? How come Hope didn't have its own box? What was it doing in a fucking box of evil?"

In a manner of speaking, Trudell sees his humanity as his religion. "There is a common spirituality which underlies nationality and race and religion and even tribe. A common reality of what it is to be human," he says. "All things have spirit—a rock, a tree, a person—and all of those things are part of a greater spiritual reality. We are all shapes of the earth. The elements in our bodies are made up of the elements of the earth. And everybody is made up of those elements. We are human beings. The physical is the 'human' part. The 'being' is our connection to the moon and the universe. I am part of a larger creation. There is something inside me that knows it. I trust my creator and my creation. But there is no 'higher power' separate from reality. Power is just part of reality.

"I have seen a lot of people who are on a spiritual quest who still just don't get it. They are seeking knowledge, but they stop at the New Age section of the bookstore. I'm not saying they're looking in the wrong place for their spirit, but they're not looking in *enough* places. They forget to look within themselves. They don't even see themselves anymore, and the first place they look is outside of themselves? It doesn't make sense. You can't be a spiritual person and sit off on the sidelines with all the bad things that are going on. It just doesn't work that way."

"No matter what they ever do to us, we must always act for the love of our people and the earth. We must not react out of hatred against those who have no sense." —John Trudell at the Black Hills Survival gathering, 1980

♥ LEARN MORE

John Trudell
www.johntrudell.com

American Indian Movement
www.aimovement.org

AIM Movement History
www.dickshovel.com/AIMIntro.html

BOOKS

Stickman
by John Trudell
(poetry)
Inanout Press, 1995

Like a Hurricane: The Indian Movement from Alcatraz to Wounded Knee
by Paul Chaat Smith and Robert Allen Warrior
New Press, 1996

In The Spirit of Crazy Horse
by Peter Matthiessen
Viking Press, 1991

Cointelpro Papers: Documents From the FBI's Secret Wars Against Domestic Dissent
by Ward Churchill and Jim Vander Wall
South End Press, 1990

ALBUMS BY JOHN TRUDELL

AKA Graffiti Man
Rykodisc (1992)

Johnny Damas and Me
Rykodisc (1994)

Blue Indians
Inside (1999)

Bone Days
Daemon Records (2001)

RIGOBERTA MENCHÚ TUM

MAYAN INDIGENOUS RIGHTS ACTIVIST

The story of Rigoberta Menchú Tum—indigenous activist, human rights leader, and winner of the 1992 Nobel Prize for Peace—cannot be separated from the story of her people, and of the civil war that ravaged Guatemala for 36 years. The death toll exceeded those of Chile, Nicaragua, El Salvador, and Argentina, combined. Of more than 200,000 people killed or disappeared, Guatemalan authorities were responsible for 85 percent of the deaths and numerous acts of genocide. Yet despite this massive bloodletting, it was not until Menchú told the story of her people's suffering that the world at large began to take notice.

Menchú was born on January 9, 1959, to a poor Mayan peasant family of the K'Iche tribe. Her parents had both converted to Catholicism, and raised their six children in the faith. While still a teenager, Rigoberta became involved in Catholic social reform programs and joined a grassroots women's-rights movement. Her family eventually become embroiled in the country's civil war, which had begun the year of Menchú's birth. The conflict had grown out of the theft of land from the Mayans by colonizing Europeans throughout the previous four centuries, and as farming Mayan peasants, the Menchús were on the wrong side of history. Accused of supporting anti-government guerrillas, her father was imprisoned, tortured, and eventually killed by Guatemalan authorities. Her brother was killed by security forces in 1979; and a year later, her mother also died after being arrested, tortured, and raped.

So much loss radicalized Menchú even further. Already, in 1979, she had joined the Committee of the Peasant Union, or CUC, but now she became more involved in the struggle, helping to organize strikes and demonstrations. She was also a member of a group called the Revolutionary Christians, mostly Mayan farmers whose forebears had been converted to Catholicism by missionaries. Menchú—like many Mayan Christians—also practiced her native K'Iche spiritual traditions, using the Mayan sacred creation story known as the Popul Vuh as a spiritual guide for her life and work.

In 1981, Menchú went into hiding, then fled to Mexico. In exile, she continued to organize resistance to the military repression. Meanwhile, in Guatemala, a coup led by Efraín Ríos Montt overthrew the U.S.–supported military dictatorship of Romeo Lucas Garcia and replaced it with his own. Ríos Montt massively escalated the violence, especially against the indigenous population.

While in exile in Paris in 1983, Menchú told her life story to anthropologist Elisabeth Burgos-Debray. The book that resulted—known in English as *I, Rigoberta Menchú: An Indian Woman in Guatemala*—brought new attention to the genocide in Guatemala, and to the money, weapons, and military training provided by the United States. Describing with eloquent simplicity the lives of the Maya, the rise of the guerrilla movement, and the brutal military repression, her book played a crucial role in mobilizing international opposition to the Guatemalan dictatorship. Menchú has become a leading advocate of indigenous people's rights and ethnic reconciliation, not just in Guatemala but throughout the hemisphere. She has received several international awards, including the 1992 Nobel Peace Prize.

LEARN MORE

The Rigoberta Menchu Foundation
A charitable organization dedicated to human-rights issues in Guatemala and other Latin American countries.
1a. Avenida 9-18, Zona 1,
Ciudad de Guatemala
Guatemala, C.A.
Tel.: (502) 250 0029
Email: frmtmexico@rigobertamenchu.org
Web site: www.rigobertamenchu.org

I, Rigoberta Menchú:
An Indian Woman in Guatemala
by Rigoberta Menchú with
Elizabeth Burgos-Debray
Verso Books, 1987

Silence on the Mountain: Stories of Terror, Betrayal, and Forgetting in Guatemala
by Daniel Wilkinson
Houghton Mifflin, 2002

Maya Resurgence in Guatemala: Q'Eqchi' Experiences
by Richard Wilson
University of Oklahoma Press, 1999

WINONA LADUKE

OJIBWE ENVIRONMENTAL AND INDIGENOUS RIGHTS ACTIVIST

Perhaps best known as the vice-presidential running mate of Green Party candidate Ralph Nader in the 1996 and 2000 U.S. presidential elections, Winona LaDuke is more activist than politician.

Born in 1959 to a Anishinaabe father (who had bit-parts playing an Indian in Hollywood Westerns) and a Jewish art professor mother, LaDuke is as complex as her heritage. She is a journalist, author, activist, organizer, orator, and mother of three.

She grew up in suburban Los Angeles and earned an economics degree from Harvard University, but settled on the White Earth reservation in Minnesota to reconnect with her roots. In the 20 years she's been there, she has helped the Ojibwe tribe buy back thousands of acres of ancestral land. She has spoken on issues of land rights, environmental racism, and indigenous women before the United Nations. She founded the Indigenous Women's Environmental Network and the Honor the Earth Fund to empower grassroots activism

ACT NOW   www.honorearth.org

among native women against, among other things, the dumping of nuclear waste on Native American lands. But it is the spiritual traditions of her tribe that sustain her. "Spirituality is the foundation of all my political work," LaDuke told *Mother Jones* magazine in 1996. "In many of the progressive movements in this country, religion carries a lot of baggage. But I think that's changing. You can't dismiss the significance of Eastern religions, earth-based religions, and Western religions on political work today. What we all need to do is find the wellspring that keeps us going, that gives us the strength and patience to keep up this struggle for a long time."

❤ LEARN MORE

Indigenous Women's Environmental Network/Honor the Earth
A national foundation and advocacy organization that supports front-line Native environmental work, with a focus on intertribal coalitions of Native women activists.
2801 21st Avenue South
Minneapolis, MN 55407
Tel.: (800) EARTH-07
Email: honorearth@earthlink.net
Web site: www.honorearth.org

The Winona LaDuke Reader: A Collection of Essential Writings
by Winona LaDuke
Voyager Press, 2002

Defending Mother Earth: Native American Perspectives on Environmental Justice
by Jace Weaver
Orbis Books, 1996

A SPARK

FOR

JUSTICE

ISABELL COE

WIRAGARIEE, ABORIGINAL TENT EMBASSY DIPLOMAT

As Isabell Coe inched her way up Glastonbury Tor, the small group awaiting her at the top of the hill had a clear view of the approaching sunset. The Tor was crowded with visitors: tourists chatting, children playing, people pausing in meditation—all waiting for the sun to set on this ancient place of pilgrimage.

The climb was a physical struggle for the 51-year-old Coe, the pain in her hips making it difficult to walk, but she was there to lead a sacred Aboriginal ceremony and would not be held back. She was bringing the eternal "fire of peace and justice"—sparked in each new ceremony with ashes from the last—to that site, itself sacred to the ancient people of England. As she reached the top, a companion arranged the eucalyptus leaves for the fire. Then, as each participant added a branch to the flames, they prayed for peace and justice for all people, for all creatures, for the whole of creation. "People from all cultures understand the fire," says Coe. "It's the most ancient ceremony there is."

But Isabell Coe's agenda goes deeper than spreading goodwill and blessings. As custodian of the Wiragariee tribe, she is calling for the war on her people to end—the war that began when the British first landed on the shores of Australia, the war that goes on today. White politicians talk about reconciliation but have done little of consequence, to Coe's mind.

ACT NOW www.eniar.org

"*Even when our people are dead, they lock up their spirits in jail. We are still fighting for sovereignty, and we are not going to go away, we will always be there.*"

—Isabell Coe

Former prime ministers like Bob Hawke and Malcolm Frazer marched across Sydney Harbor Bridge touting reconciliation in 2000, though they did nothing to right their government's injustices against Aborigines when they were in power. None of the talking, the important-sounding government panels and inquiries will bring back the Aboriginal heads dispatched around the world as war trophies, or put the spirits of Aboriginal warriors to rest. There can be no reconciliation until the war has been acknowledged, says Coe.

Then Aboriginal sovereignty must be recognized and someone must take responsibility for the injustice that has been done, she says. The ceremonial fire at Glastonbury was one of many that Coe lit on her visit to the British Isles in the autumn of 2001. She traveled from the southwest tip of England, along a route sometimes known as "the back of the dragon"—a parallel, Isabell noted,

Aborigines suffer far higher rates of poverty, disease and infant mortality than white Australians.

to the sacred Rainbow Serpent of Aboriginal spiritual tradition. She asked that the guardians of each place she visited be present, so local people joined in, adding their prayers to the fires. She visited sacred places in Wales, and in Ireland lit a fire at a chapel sacred to St. Bridget, where an eternal flame is tended by the Catholic nuns. From there, she went to Runnymede to light a fire at the site of the Magna Carta's signing—the Great Charter that made the English monarch answerable to the people of England.

There were meetings, of course, and the usual round of lobbying while Coe was in London. But for her it was bringing the fire to England—to the source of the injustice, the origin of the genocide against her people—that mattered most.

A HISTORY OF LOSS

For the Aborigines and Torres Strait Islanders of Australia—perhaps the world's oldest peoples—the arrival of Britain's newest penal colony in 1788 was a catastrophe. The convicts, soldiers, and settlers brought diseases to which the native population had no resistance: flu, smallpox, typhoid, and venereal disease. Over the ensuing century, they were driven from their own country—shot, poisoned, massacred, herded onto reserves, and forced to flee as each wave of British settlers seized more land for building, farming, grazing, and mining.

The constitution that transferred power from Great Britain to the Australian federal government in 1900 and 1901 changed almost nothing for the Aborigines. Many Aboriginal children were taken forcibly from their families to be raised—and abused—in institutions. Aborigines could not vote and essentially had no citizenship until the 1960s.

But even after 200 years of fierce oppression, the European settlers were unable to obliterate Aboriginal identity. Although through resistance Aborigines have won considerable rights and redress, the struggle continues—for land, jobs, decent health care and education, adequate water and power, and an end to the extraordinary rates of incarceration and death among Aboriginal people. And Isabell Coe continues to fight on behalf of her people—for recognition, for justice, for sovereignty.

THE TENT EMBASSY

The Aboriginal Tent Embassy was established in 1972 on the lawns of Parliament House in Canberra, the Australian federal capital, in response to a federal ruling rejecting Aboriginal land rights and instead suggesting that only temporary leases be granted to Aborigines. In its earliest days the embassy produced a list of demands for land-rights, including the legal title and mineral rights to the Aboriginal reserves, legal and political control of the entire Northwest Territory, and compensation for stolen land in the amount of $6 billion and a permanent share of federal revenues. Predictably, the demands were roundly rejected. But the embassy lived on.

With the exception of some violent confrontations in which government authorities tried forcibly to remove the tents, it has remained a permanent fixture and symbol of the Aboriginal struggle for land rights, self-determination, and sovereignty, as well as for the stubborn intractability of the Australian white ruling class. Its staying power, despite its rickety temporary architecture, has served to unite the many and disparate Aboriginal tribes across the country behind a single political cause. It has also been a thorn in the side of the Australian government, which chafes at the implications of the word "embassy"—that it

ACT NOW www.eniar.org

"We have to be honest and we can't continue down the track where we are going to make the same mistakes of the past. It's like expecting the Jewish people to celebrate and embrace what Nazi Germany did in Germany against the Jewish people." —Isabell Coe represents a sovereign nation of people who are effectively non-citizens in their own land. That's just how the embassy organizers intended it. And to drive the point home, within a month of the embassy's establishment, organizers has designed and sewn a new Aboriginal national flag to fly above the tent city. Coe has been involved in the Tent Embassy since she was a teenager, just free from the mission where she had been raised by whites. Her partner Billy Craigie (who died in 1999) was one of the embassy's original founders.

The embassy has a spiritual as well as political significance for many Aborigines, and the protests there often involve sacred rites and rituals. Sacred ceremonial sticks representing the spirits of embassy participants who have died during the struggle stand watch steadily within the tent circles. In 1998 on Australia Day, Coe lit the sacred fire of peace and justice at the embassy. It has been burning somewhere in the world ever since.

THE INTERNATIONAL STAGE

When the 2000 Olympic Games came to Sydney, a Tent Embassy was established at Victoria Park, where it provided an ironic counterpoint to the Australian government's glossy presentation of racial harmony as part of the official festivities. The sacred fire was transported to the site, and everyone from tourists and sports fans to security guards was invited to add eucalyptus branches and prayers to it; during the games, even the white Australian police turned up each day to take part.

After the games had ended, Coe led a delegation from the embassy that took possession of Cockatoo Island in Sydney Harbor. Like Alcatraz in California, Cockatoo was formerly sacred native land that had been stolen by white colonists and turned into a prison, and later a

ACT NOW   www.eniar.org

military installation. And like the American Indians who occupied Alcatraz in 1970, the Aborigines were prepared to make a symbolic stand. Upon landing at Cockatoo, Coe reenacted the rhetorical gesture of the first British invaders by declaring it *terra nullius*—land belonging to no one. Then, after a sacred smoking ritual to cleanse the island of its violent past, Coe lit the fire for peace and justice and claimed the island for Aboriginal people.

Coe and the others were evicted and found guilty of trespassing, a judgment they swiftly appealed. A high court asserted that the burden of proof of Aboriginal sovereignty lay with the defendants. In their appeal, Coe and her codefendants turned the tables, challenging the Australian courts to prove that they—functionaries of the descendants of Europeans—had sovereignty over Australia. In a logical bind, the courts responded by passing the buck, saying that only the English courts or the World Court could decide the issue.

So in 2001, Coe called their bluff.

THE WORLD COURT

She traveled first to the Hague—with a delegation in tow—to initiate a case in the World Court charging that the British and their white Australian descendants illegally stole sovereign Aboriginal lands, as well as committing acts of genocide and crimes against humanity. Coe's goal is to prove that the Aboriginal nations never ceded sovereignty.

"We have been to the highest courts in Australia over genocide and our sovereign land rights and there has been no justice," Coe said in a press release upon her arrival in the Netherlands. "We need to establish our office of the Aboriginal Tent Embassy here in the

This hill is a sacred site for the Ayiparinya (caterpillar) dreaming. It is protected under the Aboriginal Sacred sites Protection Act. In our traditional law no-one can damage this place. Please respect it. No trail bike riders allowed.

signed by Alice Springs traditional owners
Stevens & Golder & Rice Families.

Hague, so we are on neutral diplomatic ground and will be able to bring our elders and our people over to Europe to tell their stories to the World Court.

"We are here to deliver a Declaration of Aboriginal Sovereignty over the land known as Australia, and to deliver a Declaration of Peace, to end the war that has been waged against Australian Aboriginal people since Australia was invaded. We would like both the British and Australian High Commissioners to notify the British Crown and the Australian Governor General that this process has begun."

The case could have far-reaching implications in paces like Guatemala, the United States, and Canada, where new colonies and nations were founded through the elimination or subjugation of native peoples. It will be a long struggle, Coe acknowledges, but there have been some indications that the international community might be sympathetic: After all, months after the Australian government amended its land-rights laws to prevent Aborigines from claiming native title to swaths of farmland, Australia was condemned as racist by the United Nations Committee on the Elimination of Racial Discrimination. It is the only developed country ever chastised for institutional racism by the U.N. With the Tent Embassy established and the World Court litigation underway, Coe went on to the British Isles, carrying the sacred fire of peace into the land of her ancient enemy.

FIGHTING FIRE WITH SACRED FIRE

Coe knows that she must keep going. Things have gotten worse for her people, not better. Aborigines used to be buried in twos and threes; now the funerals come ten and twelve at a time, so many that Coe has to make up her mind which to attend. It's not just older people, either, but children, teenagers, people of all ages—the life expectancy of an Aborigine is about 20 years shorter than that of a white Australian. In a sense, the mistreatment of Aborigines is good for the country's economy, Coe notes ironically: federally subsidized health care, welfare support, legal assistance, and prisons for Aborigines are rapidly growing industries that support large numbers of (mostly white) Australian workers. Coe says it would be simpler just to give every man, woman, and child a million dollars—the government would still be half a billion dollars better off each year.

But she knows that the institutionalized racism disguised as compassionate public services for the underprivileged is just another form of genocide with fancy window dressing. "Now they are killing us with a stroke of a pen," she says. The Aboriginal Elders have told their people that the people of the world are hungry for peace, and Coe is committed to taking the fire ceremony wherever it is needed. She has traveled with the fire to Woolganer, where they

Conditions in heavily Aboriginal slums are among the worst in the world.

are trying to halt development on the site where the remains of a 6,000-year-old "clever man" were found. She plans to visit Sandham Point, where cyanide from mining operations is destroying the river system. She knows she must keep going, for her children, for her grandchildren, and for places like Lake Cowe in Timbaarra, where the mine was closed just one month after they conducted the fire ceremony there.

Although Coe called the government's watered-down offers "re-con-silly-ation," and is unlikely to be satisfied with any compromise short of justice, equality, and fair compensation, she continues to fight to be heard on the subject and is also willing to listen. When she returned from England in 2001, discussions about the reconciliation process were still going on in Canberra. Coe and other Aboriginal leaders marched to Parliament House, carrying the sacred fire of peace and justice and the sacred ceremonial sticks of the Tent Embassy participants who had died since 1972. They asked the politicians and bureaucrats to come outside and speak with them around the fire. The police arrived instead. In a surreal scene, the fire was taken into custody, put onto the back of a truck, and driven away. The sacred ceremonial sticks were hauled off to prison; it took a court action to get them released.

In a sense—surreal or not—this carried the genocide to its logical conclusion, says Coe: "Even when our people are dead, they lock up their spirits in jail." Then again, let them try. Isabell Coe's spirit is unbending. She will have peace, but on her terms and with the whole world watching. That's why she has never compromised her principles nor changed her tune, just as her people never ceded their homeland to the Europeans. "We are still fighting for sovereignty, and we are not going to go away," she affirms. "We will always be there."

CHARLES PERKINS

ARRENTE ABORIGINAL CIVIL-RIGHTS ADVOCATE

Charles Perkins rarely held his tongue, and never shielded anyone from truths they'd rather not see. His outspokenness on issues of Aboriginal rights would probably have been enough to win him a spot in Australian history books, but his actions made him a fixture in the national public consciousness. Dubbed "Australia's Martin Luther King Jr." and frequently equated with South Africa's Nelson Mandela, he is unquestionably the best-known native-rights activist in Australian history.

His explosive passion was instilled in Perkins early. His mother Hetti was a queen of the Arrente people, and a bona fide character: strong-willed, defiant, and quirky. She gave birth to Charlie on a tabletop in an abandoned telegraph office in Alice Springs in 1936. Although he was only half Aborigine, Perkins was still vulnerable to government agents who took children from their families and sent them to institutions in order to forcibly "assimilate" them. (Those children are now known as the "Stolen Generation.") Charlie was never taken—his mother saw to that—but the system didn't leave him unscathed: one brother committed suicide, and his sole memory of his grandmother was the image of a face behind barbed wire.

In the mid-1960s, Perkins began leading white students on freedom rides into the outback of New South Wales, much like the freedom riders in the civil-rights movement of the American South. Busloads of young volunteers traveled out to the outback and witnessed the grinding

 ACT NOW   www.reconciliationaustralia.org

"We wander through Australian society as beggars. We live off the crumbs that fall off the White Australian tables and are told to be grateful. This is what Australia Day means to Aboriginal Australians. We celebrate with you, but there is much sadness in our joy. It is like dancing on our mother's grave. We know we cannot live in the past but the past lives in us."
—Charles Perkins

conditions suffered by Aborigines on the reserves. The riders publicly demonstrated for the desegregation of public spaces, such as community swimming pools.

They were spat upon, threatened by furious white crowds, assaulted. But they began to win the occasional battle, starting with the desegregation of the swimming pool in the town of Moree in 1965. These victories brought Charles Perkins to the forefront of national attention; his talent, his outrage, his persistence, and his brilliant achievements would keep him there for the remainder of his life. In addition to being only the second Aborigine ever to graduate from an Australian university, Perkins made history upon becoming the first Aborigine ever to serve in the federal government in Canberra. He began in the Department of Aboriginal

Charles Perkins (left) was unmoved by Prime Minister John Howard's empty promises of reconciliation.

Affairs in Canberra and eventually rose to the post of permanent secretary. But he refused to behave differently in deference to the establishment, despite his new membership in it. He called Prime Minister John Howard a "dog" and a "racist" for rewriting land ownership laws to further disenfranchise Aborigines.

Charles Perkins' mission was to communicate a simple message to the world, and to his fellow Australians: The government's policies toward Aborigines have been and continue to be the literal and moral parallel of South Africa's apartheid system. Bringing tremendous courage, energy, and inventiveness to bear, he made the squalor and discrimination suffered by Aborigines visible, whether people wanted to see it or not. It earned him much enmity, but also international praise and admiration.

Of course, the Australian government had made much of its opposition to apartheid in South Africa. The 2000 Olympic Games in Sydney, too, included a deftly orchestrated public relations festival showcasing Australian "reconciliation." Perkins, who did not suffer hypocrisy quietly, pointed out that national and international bodies (including the U.N.) had found Australia guilty of fundamental human-rights breaches in its treatment of Aborigines—hardly the stuff of reconciliation.

Right up to his death, Perkins struggled for justice and dignity for his people, and provided a role model for a generation of activists, both white and Aboriginal. Perhaps his greatest gift to his people—and to white Australians as well—was this: By insisting on the truth, Charles Perkins laid the groundwork for true reconciliation.

KEVIN BUZZACOTT

ARABUNNA ELDER, ANTI-NUCLEAR ACTIVIST

For three months in 2000, Kevin "Uncle Kev" Buzzacott walked the scalding landscape of the Australian outback from his sacred tribal home on the shore of Lake Eyre in South Australia to Sydney, the site of the first colonial outpost established by the British in 1788. For Buzzacott and the hundreds of Aborigines and non-Aborigine sympathizers who joined him on the walk, the journey was a symbol of peace and an act of hope for reconciliation between his people and the white colonists who have marginalized the Aborigines and exploited their land for generations.

In 1999, Buzzacott, an elder of the Arabunna tribe and custodian of its traditions and culture, established the Arabunna Going Home Camp at Lake Eyre in South Australia. Like the Tent Embassy in Canberra, the Going Home Camp is an ad-hoc conglomeration of temporary buildings intended as a symbol of the native people's spiritual and legal claim to the land. After centuries of disenfranchisement and relocation, the Arabunna people had largely been dispersed throughout Australia by 1999; when he founded the camp, Buzzacott called on them to return to their traditional ancestral lands to defend them from destruction and exploitation. Hundreds have. Among the most sacred sites in Arabunna culture is Lake Eyre, whose water is considered so infused with significance that Aborigines are not permitted even to dip their feet into it.

ACT NOW   www.lakeeyre.green.net.au

"Is there any justice out there? When do we have access to basic human rights and the right to peacefully live in our own land? When can we go home?"
—Kevin Buzzacott

But others disputed the Arabunna claim to the water; specifically, the Western Mining Corporation, which had been granted mineral rites in the region and operates two uranium mines on what the tribe considers its ancestral territory.

One of Western's mines has a permit to use up to 42 million liters of Lake Eyre's water every day. So diminished is the local water table now, that several nearby natural springs have ebbed to nothing. Radioactive waste from the mines litters the countryside, sickening residents and poisoning the land for the foreseeable future. Now the company is proposing a nuclear dump site at Billa Kalina, also considered Arabunna tribal land.

To the Arabunna, the destruction of the lake is an affront to their spiritual freedom, and they know that they must fight back now or risk losing their land forever.

In the three years since the first tent stake was driven, officials of the mining company—with back-up from local and federal white law enforcement—have daily harassed the residents. Twice they bulldozed the camp and stole or destroyed the personal belongings of the campers. In 2000, Western Mining tried to evict the camp, claiming residents had damaged company property.

Instead of responding in anger, however, Buzzacott embarked on a mission of peace. He lit a sacred fire at the Coming Home Camp in June 2000, and carried the flame 3,060 kilometers in 85 days on foot to Sydney where the Olympic Games were being held. There he joined the Tent Embassy and added the voice of the Arabunna to the chorus for justice. "This historic walk is a journey for peace, freedom, and healing the land and its peoples," he said in a public statement along the way. "If the South Australian government refuses to act in closing down WMC at Roxby Downs and prevent the establishment of a uranium waste dump at Billa Kallina, then the looming reality of the genocide of the Arabunna people will be realized."

In 2001, Buzzacott was named a recipient of the Nuclear-Free Future Award. In his acceptance speech he said, "We are the rightful owners of this whole country. The residents of the camp are people from all over the world who have the full permission of the Arabunna nation to live in our country, unlike WMC who are the masters of oppression, the corporation of theft and the kings of genocide.

"Is there any justice out there? When do we have access to basic human rights and the right to peacefully live in our own land? When can we go home?"

LEARN MORE

The Keepers of Lake Eyre
Tel.: (08) 8340 4401
Email: lakeeyre@microsuxx.com
Web site: www.lakeeyre.green.net.au

Nuclear Free Future
A foundation promoting nuclear weapons
and energy resistance and alternatives.
www.nuclear-free.org

❤ GET INVOLVED

European Network for Indigenous Australian Rights (ENIAR)
A volunteer nonprofit that compiles news and information relating to the Aboriginal struggle for human rights and justice.
LB 723
London W1A 9LB
United Kingdom
Email: info@einar.org
Web site: www.eniar.org

Australians for Native Title
A group organizing grassroots lobbying campaigns on behalf of Aboriginal sovereignty. Includes info on the "Sorry Books," a popular movement of apology by Australian citizens responding to the government's refusal to apologize for past abuses of Aborigines.
Web site: www.nativetitle.aust.com

Australians for Native Title and Reconciliation
Another group supporting Aboriginal land rights. Includes information on the Sea of Hands campaign.
PO Box 1176
Rozelle NSW 2039
Tel.: (02) 9555 6138
Email: antar@antar.org.au
Web site: www.antar.org.au

Reconciliation Australia
A nonprofit dedicated to tracking the official process of reconciliation.
PO Box 4773
Kingston ACT 2604
Tel.: (02) 6295 9266
Email: inquiries@reconciliation.org.au
Web site: www.reconciliationaustralia.org

National Indigenous Working Group
An organization dedicated to resolution of government policy on Aboriginal land ownership.
PO Box 201
Deakin West, ACT 2600
Tel.: (61) 6234 3330
Email: niwg@faira.org.au
Web site: www.faira.org.au/niwg

THE

AMERICAN

GHANDI

A.J. MUSTE

CALVINIST-QUAKER LABOR LEADER

I t's 1896 on a winter day inside a tiny classroom in Grand Rapids, Michigan. The class clown is meekly on his way to the front of the room to be disciplined for certain "shenanigans." As he makes his way up the rows of wooden desks, out of the corner of his eye—too late—he sees a foot dart out. Before he can avoid it, his toe catches the errant ankle and he tumbles in a heap at the teacher's feet. Instead of suspecting foul play, the teacher assumes the boy was intentionally making a scene, and she doubles his punishment.

The offending ankle belonged to 11-year-old Abraham Johannes Muste, who would never really understand what, other than an adolescent tendency toward mischief, made him trip his classmate. But he would mark the moment as the unlikely beginning of his remarkable path to nonviolent activism.

After school, Muste and the furious boy met at the school perimeter, just beyond the sight of teachers and school administrators. As other boys circled around them hoping to see a fistfight, Muste stood stock still. "You tripped me," said the boy, expecting no doubt for Muste to either throw a defensive punch or run. "Yes I did," said Muste, expressionless despite his pounding heart. The boy stood dumbfounded. He hadn't expected Muste to admit his crime, let alone fail to flee from its consequences. Eventually, wordlessly, the boy turned and walked away. In his "Sketches for an Autobiography" in *The Essays of A.J. Muste* (Nat

"There is no way to peace; peace is the way."
—A.J.Muste

Hentoff, ed.; Simon & Schuster, 1970) Muste wrote that it was only 40 years later that he realized how seminal that moment was. "[I]t came home to me that it illustrated several aspects of the pacifist philosophy which I had consciously adopted in 1915 but toward which I had, no doubt, an inclination many years earlier." He notes that in that moment, he disarmed his enemy with spontaneity, imagination, and honesty. By refusing to fight or to flee, Muste had left his opponent without a reflexive reaction. And most of all, by admitting guilt and standing prepared for its consequences, Muste had gained the moral advantage. Such are the fundamental tenets of nonviolent resistance, which he would later expound in his book *Non-Violence in an Aggressive World* (Jerome S. Ozer Publishing, 1972). Without knowing it, he had discovered the power of what Daniel Berrigan would later sum up with his aphorism, "Don't just do something, stand there."

Muste would become perhaps the steadiest figure in the major social movements of the American 20th century, yet he is probably the least recognized and most misunderstood. And that may be by design. After all, he managed in his lifetime a relatively fluid transition from strictly conservative Dutch Reform minister to Marxist-Leninist, to Trotskyist, to Quaker pacifist, to "Calvinist socialist."

As a leading proponent of nonviolent resistance, he became a natural leader in both the American labor and anti-war movements, and a huge force in the civil-rights movement. Among those he took into his confidence were some of the most influential figures of the century: He collaborated with Dorothy Day and mentored Martin Luther King, Jr., in the principles and practice of nonviolent civil disobedience.

He would also win remarkable opportunities to match wits with revolutionary figures Leon Trotsky and Ho Chi Minh. He also managed—like so many prominent social activists—to be rebuked by FBI director J. Edgar Hoover, which he considered something of an honor.

Muste's total lack of ego and lack of hunger for celebrity or glory before anyone but his own God made him a shadow in the history books, though he eventually became renowned in India as "the American Gandhi." This distinguishing gift also enabled him to quickly win loyalty and trust from those who could sense he was not pushing his own agenda. But Muste first came to prominence as a unorthodox labor leader, a role he landed in accidentally and excelled at not so much through his revolutionary ideals, as through his revolutionary methods.

CALVINIST ROOTS, PACIFIST HEART

Muste was born in Holland, and moved with his family to Michigan at age 6. Everything about his childhood prepared him to be a man of the cloth, and indeed in 1909 he was ordained in the Dutch Reformed Church. But stories of the Great War reached him from across the ocean, and its brutality struck him as both tragic and morally indefensible. News of the war moved him to pacifism, which he saw as not only consistent with, but demanded by, his faith. But that put him at odds with a church that was openly endorsing U.S. involvement.

"I could not 'bend' the Sermon on the Mount and the whole concept of the Cross and suffering love to accommodate participation in war," Muste wrote in a 1957 essay.

His pacifism made him increasingly unpopular, not only with his congregation, but with his church superiors, for whom Muste's ethic of nonviolent resistance veered dangerously close to disobedience and even latent Communism. In 1916, he was forced to resign his ministry.

"It was quite an experience to be, in effect, driven out of a pulpit which for my predecessors had proved a stepping stone to highly distinguished careers in the ministry, and to find myself marked as a pacifist and a possibly dangerous character," Muste said.

Muste found solace and a natural affinity among the Quakers, who welcomed him into their Massachusetts community. Invited one day to sermonize at a Friends meeting, Muste spoke out against the United States' entry into the conflict, even as some among his congregation were being conscripted. A Baptist minister from a nearby church had sneaked into the Meeting House and was outraged by what he heard. As Muste left the meeting, a sheriff stopped him.

ACT NOW   www.ajmuste.org

"*It is often said that pacifism, or conscientious objection to war, is based upon a literalistic use of the command, 'Thou shalt not kill,' as if it were an order from outside oneself, an easy rule with which to dispose of a complex problem. There have been pacifists of whom that could be said. But is there not behind the commandment of stone or of paper a command written on the heart issuing from the heart's own awareness of the preciousness, the wonder of all life and the consequent irrationality and pity of anything that wounds and mutilates a living creature and needlessly snuffs out its life, which issues in that 'reverence for life' to which Albert Schweitzer has summoned this generation so horribly addicted to violence?*"

—A. J. Muste

The sheriff, with the Baptist minister at his side, demanded to know exactly what Muste had said, because the Baptist has reported Muste's sermon as "treasonous." Since no one on the scene seemed willing or able to reproduce Muste's sermon verbatim, the sheriff reluctantly let him go.

Muste's opinion of the war became moot when it ended in 1918; but he had paid a price for his convictions, and was eager to see if the sacrifice was indeed meaningful. He worried that his opposition to the war had been largely symbolic; he and his fellow pacifists had spoken out against the war, sometimes at great professional and social risk, but none of them had ever truly risked their lives or had their philosophy of nonviolence tested. They were about to.

THE LAWRENCE STRIKE

As Muste became more deeply involved with the Quakers of Boston, there erupted in the New England region a series of turbulent labor disputes in the textile factories. Energies the Quaker community had previously reserved for anti-war activities were soon channeled into labor organizing. Muste quickly discovered that he was in his element, and that many of the principles that had guided his pacifist ideology not only applied to the labor movement, but would actually serve to unite it.

In Lawrence, Massachusetts, the only game in town was textiles, and the mills in the town employed at least one member of nearly every family living inside the city limits, most of them poor immigrants from Ireland and Eastern Europe, about half of them women and children. (A study conducted later found that more than a third of the people employed at the mills died by age 25.) In 1912, Lawrence had been the site of a well-known strike led by the theatrical Wobblies (International Workers of the World), which had brought the mills to a

ACT NOW   www.ajmuste.org

standstill and won desperately needed improvements to working conditions, hours, and wages. But by the end of that strike, one picketer and a 15-year-old boy were dead.

By 1919, tensions were rising again among the workers in Lawrence's textile mills. Unemployment was high, and mill owners were taking advantage by enacting deep wage cuts for the 30,000 workers. The American Federation of Labor (the A.F. of L.) had refused to support a general strike, and the laborers were left to seek help from any sympathetic neighbors they could find. They called upon the local religious community, including Muste and several other members of a loose federation of clergy who had lost their ministries during the war because of their pacifism. None of them had any experience in labor disputes, but they accepted an invitation to witness a strike committee meeting. Muste was present as the committee voted to strike.

Local police and state militia feared that a labor uprising in Massachusetts would signal the beginning of a Bolshevik revolution in America. So when picketers arrived at the mills early one Sunday morning, they were beaten bloody by police and state militia called out by the mayor and the governor at the behest of the mill owners. The workers were injured and demoralized, and quickly dispersed to nearby safe-houses and hospitals. The strike committee, seeing its first effort fail and morale dipping perilously, promptly appointed Muste president and left it to him to fashion a strategy that might succeed.

Muste did what no other labor leader had done in all of Lawrence's upheavals: He decided to place himself and the other new leaders at the front of the picket line. They would stand between several thousand striking immigrants and the militia's clubs and bayonets. But

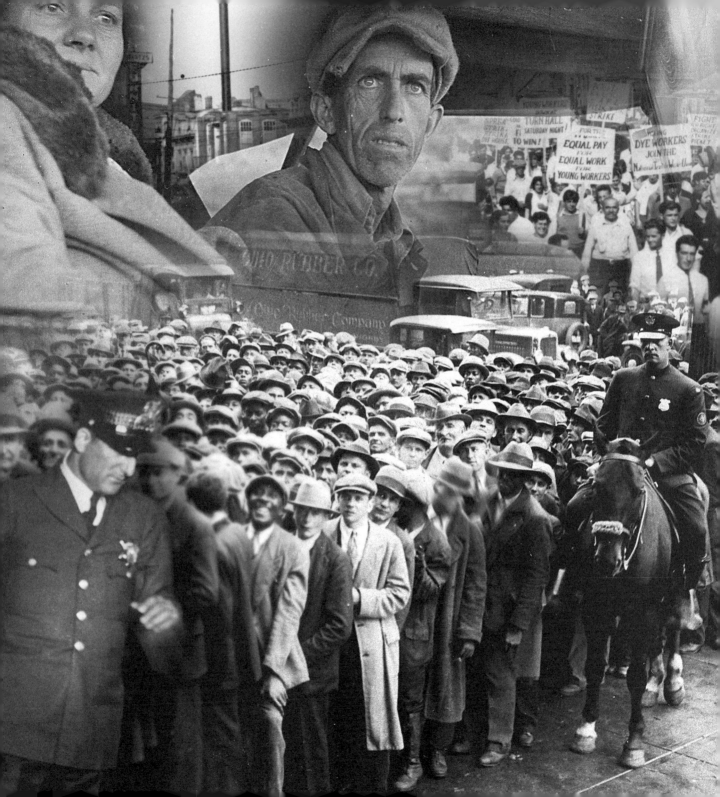

before they did so, they planned an all-hands strike-committee meeting and made sure that local police knew where and when it would be held.

Knowing there were spies in the audience, Muste delivered a sermon on nonviolence to the strikers. He insisted as a condition of his appearance at the head of the line that under no circumstances could any striker allow himself to be incited to counter-violence against the rampaging police. If they were clubbed, they were not to fight back. It was a hard sell for obvious reasons, but once it was agreed, the meeting was adjourned. Muste knew that the spies in the audience would carry back to the police news of the picketers' nonviolent intentions. It was what one of Muste's colleagues described as a moment of "moral jiu-jitsu"; the police would not be able to justify their own violence if the plan held.

Of course, the police would try. As the marchers calmly approached the site of the picket, Muste led the procession. All were silent and peaceful; the police charged up on horseback as if to quell a mob and were irritated (though probably not surprised) to find no chaos into which to dive.

Infuriated, several officers took care to cut Muste and the other leaders off from the rest of the picketers and lead them into a dark alleyway, where what happened next could not be witnessed. Muste was beaten steadily with a club and threatened repeatedly with trampling by the police mounts. He did not fight back. Eventually, he dropped to the ground from exhaustion and loss of blood. He was arrested and jailed on a charge of disturbing the peace. The strike committee bailed him out, he was acquitted (there had been no witnesses other than the police who had done the beating), and suddenly he was a hero.

The temptation to take up arms against the police was great, especially as officers mounted machine guns at the major intersections of Lawrence's working-class neighborhood. But Muste's actions had demonstrated to the strikers the power of refusing to fight fire with fire; their morale was boosted, and so was the credibility of their cause. Muste told them, "The guns were put there to provoke us: Why play into the hands of the mill management and police? It would only discredit the strike. They can't weave wool with machine guns. All we have to do is continue to stand together." The strikers eventually won; the mills had to make peace in order to stay in business. And Muste's doubts about the practical applications of pacifism evaporated.

THE TROTSKY YEARS AND BEYOND

Muste's success in Lawrence made him a celebrity and further radicalized him. In the following 10 years he would help found the largest textile workers' union in the United States, organize dozens of strikes for humane working conditions and wages, and try to revolutionize the union movement from within.

But Muste drifted away from both his pacifism and his faith in the late 1920s and early 1930s. It was then, as the Depression brought absolute desperation to the American working class, that Muste veered in and out of Communism. He was instrumental in establishing the American Workers Party, and would later merge the group with the Trotskyist movement to form the Trotskyist Workers' Party of America. But the godlessness of the American Communist movement left Muste feeling empty. Unsure about his path, he met with Leon Trotsky in Norway in 1936. It's unclear what happened at that meeting, but on his return Muste abandoned the Trotskyists and again embraced Christian pacifism.

ACT NOW   www.ajmuste.org

From 1940 to 1953, Muste served as director of the Fellowship of Reconciliation, where he again ignited controversy, first with his opposition to World War II, and later with his assistance in establishing the first militant black civil-rights organization in the south, the Congress for Racial Equality. He befriended and mentored Martin Luther King, who would use Muste's lessons to tremendous advantage in his public protests of the 1960s.

Muste was also among the first to organize the religious community in opposition to the Vietnam war. Labor disputes, civil-rights marches, or war protests, through it all Muste stayed true to those Gandhian principles of nonviolence. Other anti-war and civil-rights organizers, such as Daniel and Philip Berrigan and Malcolm X, would stray from that absolutist vision, but Muste himself never wavered.

A.J. Muste's contemporaries— including Leon Trotsky, Ho Chi Minh, and Karl Marx—influenced, but could not define him.

During the darkest days of the Vietnam war, A.J. Muste stood like a lone sentinel in front of the White House, holding a candle every night for weeks on end. According to an article by Andrea Ayvazian in *Sojourners*, one evening, a curious reporter approached and asked him, "Mr. Muste, do you really think you are going to change the policies of this country by standing out here alone at night with a candle?"

"Oh, I don't do this to change the country," Muste replied.
"I do this so the country won't change me."

LEARN MORE

A.J. Muste Memorial Institute
339 Lafayette Street,
New York, NY 10012
Tel.: (212) 533-4335
Email: ajmusteinst@igc.org
Web site: www.ajmuste.org

The Essays of A.J. Muste
Edited by Nat Hentoff
Simon & Schuster, 1970

Peace Agitator: The Story of A.J. Muste
by Nat Hentoff
A.J. Muste Memorial Institute, 1982

Abraham Went Out: A Biography of A.J. Muste
by Jo Ann Robinson
Temple University Press, 1982

World Task of Pacifism
by A.J. Muste
Pendle Hill Publications, 1942

A.J. Muste, Pacifist & Prophet: His Relation to the Society of Friends
by Jo Ann Robinson
Pendle Hill Publications, 1982

CESAR CHAVEZ

FOUNDER, UNITED FARM WORKERS

Cesar Chavez, the child of migrant farm workers, spent much of his childhood moving with his family from one California valley to the next, looking for work in the vast agricultural expanses. As an adult in 1953, Chavez and his new wife settled in a neighborhood of San Jose, California, dubbed "Sal si Puedes," which translates as "Get Out if You Can." The claustrophobic network of streets was littered with ramshackle houses too far gone even to be condemned. It was here that Chavez met a young Catholic priest who would change his life, and the lives of thousands of migrant farm workers, forever.

Chavez, who ultimately founded the United Farm Workers union, said it was Father Donald McDonnell who sparked his political and spiritual education. "We had long talks about farm workers," Chavez later recalled in Cletus E. Daniel's "Cesar Chavez and the Unionization of California Farm Workers," which appeared in *Labor Leaders in America* (Melvyn Dubofsky and Warren Van Tine, eds.; Urbana: University of Illinois Press, 1987). "I knew a lot about the work, but I didn't know anything about economics, and I learned quite a bit from him. He had a picture of a worker's shanty and a picture of a grower's mansion; a picture of a labor camp and a picture of a high-priced building in San Francisco owned by the same grower. When things were pointed out to me, I began to see... Everything he said was aimed at ways to solve the injustice." "[Father McDonnell] sat with me past midnight telling me about social justice and the Church's stand on farm labor and reading from the encyclicals of Pope Leo XIII in which he

ACT NOW   www.ufw.org

"An organizer's job is to
help ordinary people
do extraordinary things."
—Cesar Chavez

upheld labor unions. I would do anything to get the father to tell me more about labor history.
I began going to the bracero camps with him to help with Mass, to the city jail with him to
talk to prisoners, anything to be with him so that he could tell me more about the farm labor
movement." McDonnell introduced Chavez to a number of prophets of conscience—
including Gandhi and Dorothy Day-who made huge impressions and shaped Chavez's
personal and political philosophy. Chavez never strayed far

from his Catholic roots, infused though they were with Gandhian nonviolence. He rallied hundreds of thousands of migrant workers—most of them illegal immigrants and all of them abused, neglected, and exploited by wealthy agricultural concerns that operated with impunity.

And as they marched on the California State Capitol, or walked out on their jobs at great personal risk and loss, these peaceful but powerful processions often reverberated with Mexican folk chants and Christian prayers.

 # LEARN MORE

United Farm Workers of America
PO Box 62
Keene, CA 93531
Tel.: (661) 823-6252
Email: euranday@ufwmail.com
Web site: www.ufw.org

Cesar Chavez Foundation
634 S. Spring St., Ste. 727
Los Angeles, CA 90014
Tel.: (213) 362-0267
Email: cecf@ufwmail.com
Web site: www.cesarchavezfoundation.org

The National Farm Worker Ministry
438 N. Skinker Blvd.
St. Louis, MO 63130
United States
Tel.: (314) 726-6470
Email: nfwm@aol.com
Web site: www.nfwm.org

The Catholic Labor Network
A Web-based network of resources and news about Catholic and interfaith labor activism.
www.catholiclabor.org

MOTHER JONES

CATHOLIC LABOR AGITATOR

Mary Harris "Mother" Jones was to miners in the early 1900s what Cesar Chavez was to migrant farm workers in California in the 1970s and 1980s—a charismatic character inspired by her Catholic faith to give focus and vibrancy to what would become a legendary labor movement. Yet her name has practically disappeared from history books and popular memory, except as the title of a progressive magazine in America.

If nothing else, Jones was a survivor, and she discovered in herself a gift for leading others through the darkest times. She was raised in abject poverty in Ireland in a strict Roman Catholic family. The first 30 years of her life were a desperate personal struggle marked by tragedy: She lost her husband and four children to yellow fever when she was still in her 20s, then miraculously escaped with her life from the Great Fire in Chicago in 1871. Alone and with every reason to be angry with her God, she searched for a purpose above her own trials.

By the turn of the century, she had found a new voice. Strengthened and educated by her own tribulations, she fashioned herself as the matriarch of the working class in America. She emerged from nowhere in her antique black dresses and massive silk hats to lead the poor and exploited. One of her best-known actions was leading a 125-mile march of child workers from Pennsylvania textile mills to President Theodore Roosevelt's vacation home on Long

ACT NOW   www.motherjones.com

THE MOST DANGEROUS
WOMAN IN AMERICA

"Pray for the dead, and fight like hell for the living." — Mother Jones

Two child
workers in a
West Virginia
coal mine
circa 1908

Island to bring attention to the cruelty of child labor. She wasn't known for subtlety, but rather for her rousing speeches, and a gift for what today we call the "sound bite." Once, when introduced to a crowd as "a great humanitarian," she corrected the speaker: "I'm a hell-raiser!"

Jones lent her eccentric, grandmotherly charisma and growing fame to labor causes across the United States. She was among the leaders of the United Mine Workers, the Socialist Party, and the Wobblies; she organized coal and copper miners, bottle washers, steelworkers, and streetcar operators.

A district attorney in West Virginia on the other side of the coal-miners' labor struggle once called her "the most dangerous woman in America." She took it as a compliment.

"No matter what the fight, don't be ladylike! God almighty made women and the Rockefeller gang of thieves made the ladies."—Mary Harris "Mother" Jones

❤ LEARN MORE

Mother Jones Magazine
A progressive news magazine named after Mary Harris Jones.
www.motherjones.com

Mother Jones: The Most Dangerous Woman in America
by Eliott J. Gorn
Hill & Wang, 2001

THE KING

OF KINDNESS

VINOBA BHAVE

BRAHMAN LAND-RIGHTS LEADER

When Mahatma Gandhi was gunned down by a Hindu fanatic on January 30, 1948, India's hard-won independence was just 168 days old. Gandhi's followers had hoped the departure of the British would usher in an era of peace and prosperity. Instead, India was in chaos, its beloved spiritual leader was gone, and the man he had hand-picked to succeed him, Vinoba Bhave, was left with the monumental task of upholding Gandhi's principles of unity, justice, and nonviolence under trying circumstances. He would accomplish it, in part, by walking almost every square mile of India.

When British rule came to an end in August of 1947, the Indian flag was raised over a country already riven by sectarian violence. "At the stroke of the midnight hour, when the world sleeps, India will awake to life and freedom," Jawaharlal Nehru, the new nation's first Prime Minister, had said on the eve of independence. "We end today a period of ill fortune, and India discovers herself again."

But British imperialism had left behind unremitting religious warfare, unmitigated contempt for the masses by India's ruling castes, and unforgiving poverty in the countryside, where the vast majority of India's people—many of them landless peasants—tried to eke out a living. Although the country had been partitioned into two independent nations—the predominantly Hindu India and overwhelmingly Muslim Pakistan—religious hatred and brutality was still

ACT NOW   www.mkgandhi-sarvodaya.org

"I have had very sacred experiences, for I have become aware of the great purity of heart to be found among ordinary people, and have realized what a strength this is to our country." —Vinoba Bhave

rampant. Meanwhile, crushing poverty had made the Communist Party's call for armed revolution attractive to some.

Faced with this bleak state of affairs, Gandhi's most ardent followers were dispirited, but not without hope. After Gandhi's death, the movement he had led split in two. The political wing, its central goal of independence from Great Britain now achieved, aligned itself with Nehru and the new Indian state. Followers of revolutionary Gandhiism—with far broader aims, both social and spiritual—were led by the Mahatma's spiritual heir: Vinoba Bhave. Vinoba was so revered that Gandhi himself had told him, "I am not fit to measure your worth." The two men had worked together for 32 years. For 34 years more, Vinoba steadfastly worked to advance the spiritual and social revolution that Gandhi had begun.

Vinoba Bhave (left) and his mentor, Mohandas Gandhi

A SEEKER FINDS HIS DESTINY

Born on September 11, 1895, to a devout Brahmin family near Bombay, Vinoba Bhave spent his youth torn between two possible futures: the path of a spiritual seeker in the Himalayas or that of a revolutionary fighting to oust India's British rulers.

His first encounters with Gandhi in 1916 gave him the answer he sought. After reading a newspaper account of one of Gandhi's speeches, Vinoba was so taken by Gandhi's ideas that he struck up a correspondence with him. Soon Gandhi summoned the young man to his ashram and changed his life. "When I was in Kashi, my main ambition was to go to the Himalayas," Vinoba later wrote in his memoir, *Moved by Love* (Green Books, 1996). "Also there was an inner longing to visit Bengal. But neither of the two dreams could be realized. Providence took me to Gandhiji and I found in him not only the peace of the Himalayas but also the burning fervor of resolution, typical of Bengal. I said to myself that both of my desires had been fulfilled." Gandhi's example convinced Vinoba that spiritual purity and social transformation were compatible aims, and helped him realize that neither one could be achieved without the other.

Vinoba, like Gandhi, would grow to see independence as a vital step in India's evolution, but not the ultimate goal. Both men sought to weaken colonialism from within through a spiritual resistance. Both sought a social revolution that would eradicate poverty and exploitation, leaving the evils of the caste system as merely a bitter memory. The British would have to be expelled, but India must also be remade—without the fear, division, and dependence that gave the oppressors their power over the hearts and minds of the people.

SACRIFICE FOR SARVODAYA

Vinoba began his career as a freedom fighter resisting two adversaries: the caste system and the British. British rulers had little patience for Indians who objected to their presence, and Vinoba saw his share of jail cells. Gandhi sent Vinoba to Wardha Ashram in 1921, and four years later chose him to lead the Flag Satyagraha, a campaign of resistance to the British. But before he could begin, he was jailed for one month.

As soon as he was released, he resumed his leadership role and was, to no one's surprise, jailed again, this time for four months. Again he was released, again he left for Satyagraha, and yet again he was jailed—this time for a year. He rejected his jailers' attempts to give him special treatment, opting instead to do hard labor with the other inmates. Freed from prison once more, Vinoba went to Vykon in Kerala to fight for the right of Harijan (lower caste) Indians to enter the temples.

His prison experiences didn't end there. In 1932, for protesting against British rule in his writings, Vinoba was jailed for six months at Dhulia, where he gave lectures on Hindu scripture to his fellow prisoners. In October of 1940, Gandhi introduced Vinoba to the Indian public as his chosen representative on nonviolent resistance to war, who was to kick off a great campaign of civil disobedience in the struggle against the British.

As a result of his newly elevated profile, he was jailed three times in 1940 and 1941 for resistance to British rule, spending about two years behind bars. In 1942, his role in the Quit India Movement earned him another three years. After India won its independence, Vinoba continued to work for a higher goal: Sarvodaya, a society without violence and dedicated to

ACT NOW   www.mkgandhi-sarvodaya.org

THE PRICE OF RESISTANCE: VINOBA BHAVE'S TIME IN JAIL

1925 - One month for leading a campaign of resistance to British rule

|||/

1925 - Four months of resistance

|||| |||| ||

1925-26 - One year

1932 - Six months
|||| |

1940 and 1941 - A total of two years for nonviolent resistance to war

|||| |||| |||| |||| ||||

1942 - Three years for involvement in the Quit India Movement

|||| |||| |||| |||| |||| |||| |||| |

the welfare of all. The more he traveled through India, the clearer it was that independence would not cure the country's ills—least of all for India's millions of landless peasants. So he set to work establishing schools and leprosy shelters and rural development projects. He campaigned, as Gandhi had, for an end to untouchability. And, most importantly, he launched a campaign for land reform that would occupy him for the remainder of his life.

THE BHOODAN MOVEMENT

It began in 1951, on a visit to a village in Telegana. It had become evident that India's promised land reforms would not arrive on schedule, if they arrived at all, and the frustration in the countryside was reaching an extreme pitch. Wealthy landlords were being murdered. Socialists were demanding compulsory land redistribution.

When a group of landless peasants approached Vinoba to ask for his assistance, he was struck by a sudden inspiration. Addressing the village, Vinoba asked if anyone present could help. To the great surprise of the assembled villagers, one successful farmer immediately stepped forward and offered to hand over a hundred acres of his own land. This farmer's generosity planted a seed in Vinoba's mind that continued to grow for three decades, inspiring what would be known as the Bhoodan ("land gift") movement.

From that day forward, Vinoba walked from village to village—literally thousands of miles, all on foot—asking landholders to contribute land for the poor. "If you have five children," he would say, "think of me, the representative of the landless, as your sixth." In the first seven weeks, he collected more than twelve hundred acres. Others collected another hundred thousand on the movement's behalf. By 1954, the land collected had reached 2.5 million

ACT NOW www.mkgandhi-sarvodaya.org

acres, a quantity far beyond that achieved by any government land reform.

Having begun by gathering individual gifts of land, Vinoba raised the stakes with the next phase of his movement. The Gramdan ("village gift") movement asked entire villages to embrace the ideals of Sarvodaya, pledging to hold all land in trust for the community's benefit. By 1970, 160,000 villages—nearly a third of the villages in India—were participating.

By the middle of the decade, however, it had become apparent that a limit was being reached. Many landowners were donating land that was useless for agriculture, or failing to deliver on their promises at all. Faced with this collapsing momentum, Vinoba insisted on preserving the strictly voluntary character of the movement, despite the observation by more secular-minded souls (often invoking Gandhi's memory) that a campaign of active resistance might actually produce land reform with teeth.

"There is no greater weapon than the faith we place in fellow men," Vinoba replied. Vinoba did not expect this movement to put an end to the inequities of Indian society, nor even to resolve the issue of land reform itself. In this as in so any things, he aimed principally at a spiritual transformation of the hearts of the Indian people.

While the material successes of the Bhoodan movement were not inconsequential to him, neither were they his measure of success. "We do not aim at doing mere acts of kindness," he wrote, "but at creating a Kingdom of Kindness." This somewhat ethereal goal was a long way from satisfying everyone. And, the movement's astonishing successes notwithstanding, Vinoba never quite reached his target of gathering 20 million hectares of land. By the time of his voluntary death by fasting in 1982 at the age of 87, Vinoba's focus had shifted almost exclusively to the spiritual plane.

Vinoba had been a lifelong scholar with a special fascination for the spiritual traditions of both his country and the world beyond. According to Satish Kumar, who walked with Vinoba for three years through the Indian countryside, he was a great student of the major world religions. "He had studied Arabic and knew the Koran very well, and he had studied the Bible," Kumar told *In Context* magazine in 1987. "He was a great scholar of Buddhism, and he had translated Buddhist scriptures and given discourses on religions like Christianity, Hinduism, Buddhism."

Vinoba's lectures on the Upanishads and the Bhagavad Gita are considered modern religious classics. In a collection entitled *Talks on Gita* (Greenleaf Books, 1983), Vinoba writes, "My heart and mind have both received more nourishment from the Gita than my body has from my mother's milk. Where the heart is touched, there is no room for argument. Leaving logic behind, I beat the twin wings of faith and practice and, to the best of my ability, fly up into the heavens of the Gita."

Even with all that he attempted and achieved, Vinoba Bhave's greatest legacy may be the army of committed activists he left behind. In the words of Mahadev Desai, Gandhi's assistant, "Perhaps none of Gandhi's followers has created so many worshippers of truth and nonviolence, so many genuine workers, as Vinoba Bhave."

 # LEARN MORE

Bombay Sarvodaya Mandal
A charitable trust based in Bombay, the Sarvodaya conducts seminars, workshops, youth camps and compiles historical resources relating to Gandhi and Vinoba Bhave.
299, Tardeo Road, Nana Chowk
Bombay 400 007
India
Tel.: 91-22-3872061
Email: info@mkgandhi-sarvodaya.org
Web site: www.mkgandhi-sarvodaya.org

The Intimate and the Ultimate
by Vinoba Bhave, edited by Satish Kumar
Harper Collins UK, 1991

Moved by Love:
The Memoirs of Vinoba Bhave
by Vinoba Bhave, edited by Kalindi
Green Books, 1996

Talks on the Gita
by Vinoba Bhave
Greenleaf Books, 1983

Vinoba Bhave on Self-Rule and Representative Democracy
by Michael Sonnleitner
South Asia Books, 1989

SATISH KUMAR

JAIN MONK, WALKER FOR PEACE

At the age of nine, when most boys are playing soccer, learning multiplication tables, and glaring edgily at the opposite sex, Satish Kumar renounced the world and became a wandering Jain monk. This precocious spiritualism would culminate in an 8,000-mile pilgrimage for peace from India to America, through deserts, mountains, storms, and snow. And he would do it without money or shoes, entirely on foot.

Born to a deeply religious family in a tiny village in Rajastan, young Satish had long been fascinated by the Jain monks' austerity: barefoot and homeless, moving through the world with three begging bowls, the clothes on their backs, and little else. This austerity is rooted in an intense respect for life in all its forms—a respect so unstinting that a Jain walking in a dark room will sweep the ground before him with a small, soft broom lest he unwittingly crush some insect.

Despite his youth, the boy found this way of life irresistible. For the next nine years, he made it his own—studying Sanskrit, meditating for hours each day, and going once a day to beg for food. He assimilated the Jains' nonviolence and their profoundly ecological conception of humanity's place in the world. But after nine years of inwardness, he found himself dissatisfied: "I felt that my life was lacking in balance. I was pursuing the inner path at the expense of the rest of my being and the rest of the world." Kumar was ripe for a

ACT NOW resurgence.gn.apc.org

"I thought, if I walk from India to Moscow, and then walk to Paris, and then walk to London, and then walk from New York to Washington D.C., then at least I have put my body on the line, so to speak. I have put my body where my mouth is and expressed my protest by walking."
—Satish Kumar

metamorphosis when two unexpected encounters impelled him to leave the monkhood and set him on an extraordinary path. The first was a passage in a book by Gandhi, in which he maintained that the inner, religious journey and the outer, social journey should not be separated. The second was Vinoba Bhave. Though Gandhi was gone, Bhave was very much alive and the land-gift movement was in full swing.

"It was a tremendously exciting time," Kumar later said, "because thousands of people—doctors, lawyers, students, professors, businessmen—left their work and joined Vinoba." Kumar joined him too, and walked with him for three years—years of intense learning about politics, religion, and the society and culture of India, which continued after Kumar joined one of Vinoba's ashrams to study and work the land. It was while on the road with Vinoba that Kumar was inspired to walk for peace.

The year was 1961, and campaigns against nuclear weapons had mushroomed in the United States, in England, and across Europe. One day Kumar saw that Lord Bertrand Russell, a pillar of the British establishment, had gotten himself carted off to jail at the age of 90 for committing civil disobedience.

Moved and inspired by Russell's gutsy defiance, Kumar conceived an audacious plan: He, too, would put his body on the line, expressing his protest against the horror of nuclear weapons by journeying on foot from India to Moscow, Paris, and London, then continuing from New York to Washington, D.C.—all told, a distance of some 8,000 miles.

On foot, with no money in their pockets, Kumar and a colleague set out from Gandhi's grave in Delhi to bring the world a message of peace. After crossing Pakistan, Afghanistan, and Iran (where Kumar discussed disarmament with the Shah), the two men spent four months walking through the Soviet Union. At the Kremlin, they met with the Chairman of the Supreme Soviet and were given a letter of welcome from Premier Nikita Krushchev—who, preoccupied at the time with the Cuban missile crisis, was unable to greet them personally.

They walked through Poland, East and West Germany, Belgium, and France, crossing the English Channel to Dover, then continuing on foot to London. From Southampton they took a boat to New York and made their way to Washington, D.C.

By the time they arrived at the White House, it was winter. President Kennedy had been dead a little more than a month. After meeting with President Johnson's Special Advisor on Disarmament, the two men proceeded to the Arlington National Cemetery.

Having begun at the tomb of Gandhi, Kumar's trek ended at Kennedy's grave. They had walked halfway around the world preaching peace but, in the midst of the Cold War, that goal still seemed remote. Still for Satish Kumar, at least, their walk for peace had confirmed Vinoba Bhave's lifelong premise: True peace would come not when governments decreed it, but when people's hearts desired and demanded it.

❤ LEARN MORE

Resurgence
Satish Kumar and his wife June Mitchell edit this magazine on sustainable development.
Web site: http://resurgence.gn.apc.org

No Destination: An Autobiography
by Satish Kumar
Green Books, 1992

Path without Destination: The Long Walk of a Gentle Hero
by Satish Kumar
Eagle Brook, 2000

The Intimate and the Ultimate
Vinoba Bhave and Satish Kumar
Harper Collins UK, 1991

The Schumacher Lectures
Satish Kumar, editor
Little Brown UK, 1986

VANDANA SHIVA

HINDU ANTI-GLOBALIZATION ACTIVIST

With a master's degree in particle physics, a Ph.D. in the philosophy of science, and eleven books to her credit, Vandana Shiva is nothing if not erudite. But she's no ivory-tower intellectual. In 1982, several years after getting her Ph.D., she cut short her research at the Indian Institute of Management in Bangalore to establish the Research Foundation for Science, Technology, and Ecology in her home town in the Himalayan foothills. As the foundation's director, she helps communities counter threats to forests and agricultural land, leads the Navdanya ("nine seeds") movement for the conservation of indigenous seeds, and is an active and articulate defender of diversity—biological, cultural, and intellectual.

Hers is also a key voice in the international debate over globalization and development. Shiva has been an important figure in the movement to put pressure on the World Bank, the International Monetary Fund, and the World Trade Organization.

ACT NOW   www.vshiva.net

"Our policy work simultaneously addresses biodiversity, intellectual property rights, and globalization," she explains. Indeed, in 1993, Shiva won the prestigious Right Livelihood Award (referred to as the "alternative Nobel Prize") "for placing women and ecology at the heart of modern development discourse." Shiva's ecological activism began in the 1970s with the Chipko ("embrace") movement, a broad-based grassroots protest—organized principally by women—against the commercial exploitation of Himalayan forests. The women chained themselves to tree trunks or threw their arms around native trees to save them from the axe.

Shiva has taken pains ever since to draw out the connections between the environmental, the ethical, and the political. Just as Gandhi and Bhave fused the spiritual and the social in the practice of satyagraha ("fight for truth"), Shiva sees ecology and equity as a satyagraha in the same tradition. Her primary focus is on resisting the forces of globalization in India, especially agribusiness. Farmers are plunged into debt and beholden to multinational companies while the land is quickly exhausted and misery mounts.

"The real issue, for both people and nature," says Shiva, "is the extent to which control over seeds and other genetic materials is becoming increasingly concentrated in the hands of those whose only interest is profits." Shiva helps farmers roll back this process in practical ways—establishing living seed banks, training farmers in chemical-free methods of sustainable agriculture, and engaging in policy advocacy to oppose implementation of the General Agreement on Tariffs and Trade (GATT) in Indian law. This question of control is also the linchpin that links the fight for biodiversity with the defense of cultural diversity and diversity of knowledge. And it *is* a fight, albeit a nonviolent one. "The primary threat to nature and to people today comes from centralizing and monopolizing power and control," she said as she accepted the Right Livelihood award. "Not until diversity is made the logic of production will there be a chance for sustainability, justice, and peace. Cultivating and conserving diversity is no luxury in our times: It is a survival imperative."

When change comes, Shiva says it will be driven by a spiritual outrage at the brutality of corporate rule. "To be outraged by violation and violence is a necessary complement to being spiritual," she told an organic farming convention. "To me this means that one has boundaries that say, 'This is sacred, it cannot be violated.' If the rage is directed to protecting the sacred, it can become a creative rage, it can be a compassionate rage." Here, as elsewhere in Vandana Shiva's thinking, the legacy of satyagraha is legible: "From Gandhi we have learned that you cannot respond to violent systems with violence. But you have a duty to not cooperate with violence through nonviolent means."

❤ LEARN MORE

Research Foundation for Science, Technology, and Ecology
Founded in 1982 by Vandana Shiva, the Foundation is commited to conservation and the resistance of global exploitation of local ecological assets.

60, Hauz Khas
New Delhi India 110016
Tel.: +91-11-6968077
Email: vshiva@giasdl01.vsnl.net.in
Web site: www.vshiva.net

❧ GET INVOLVED

M.K. Gandhi Institute for Nonviolence
The Institute, founded by Mahatma Gandhi's grandson Arun Gandhi, was established to promote and teach the philosophy and practice of nonviolence.
c/o Christian Brothers University
650 East Parkway, South
Memphis, TN 38104
United States
Tel.: (901) 452-2824
Email: questions@gandhiinstitute.org
Web site: www.gandhiinstitute.org

Mahatma Gandhi Canadian Foundation for World Peace
An Alberta-based charity promoting Gandhi's principles of justice and nonviolence through educational grants.
P.O. Box 60002
Edmonton, Alberta
Canada
T6G 2S4
Tel.: (780) 492-5504
Fax: (780) 492-0113
Email: info@gandhi.ca
Web site: www.gandhi.ca

In the Footsteps of Gandhi: Conversations with Spiritual Social Activists
by Catherine Ingram
Parallax Press, 1990

Gandhi Today: The Story of Mahatma Gandhi's Successors
by Mark Shepard
Simple Productions, Seven Locks Press, 1987

Gandhians in Contemporary India: The Vision and the Visionaries
by Ishwar C. Harris
Edwin Mellen Press, 1998

Handbook for Satyagrahis: A Manual for Volunteers of Total Revolution
by Narayan Desai
Gandhi Peace Foundation
and Movement for a New Society, 1980

Gandhi on Non-Violence
by Mohandas Gandhi and Thomas Merton
W. W. Norton, 1965

TRUTH IN

LOVE

RELENTLESSLY

REV. MEL WHITE

EVANGELICAL CHRISTIAN GAY-RIGHTS ADVOCATE

Twenty years ago, Rev. Mel White was highly sought after among the powerful leadership of the then-burgeoning religious right movement in America. He had just finished ghostwriting Jerry Falwell's autobiography *If I Should Die Before I Wake!* when in 1985 he was urgently called to the side of another powerful evangelist, Pat Robertson. Robertson needed a ghostwriter to whip out an autobiography in time for the announcement that Robertson would run for president of the United States in 1988.

When White finished Robertson's *America's Dates with Destiny*, he was again whisked away; this time, to meet with televangelists Jim and Tammy Faye Bakker, who were planning a book on their own life stories. Mel White was quite literally the voice of the Christian conservative movement at its peak. A rising star in a rising movement, White enjoyed a full schedule writing books and speeches for the Christian right's biggest celebrities in the 1980s, including Falwell, Robertson, the Bakkers, Col. Oliver North, and Rev. Billy Graham. With a wife and two children at home, a number of bestselling books written under his own name and dozens of prize-winning evangelical films to his credit, Mel White was by all accounts blessed. He was also gay.

None of his clients knew it then, largely because White was still deeply in denial about it himself. He had spent a quarter-century fighting his homosexuality, which various pastors and

"God gave me my sexuality as a gift, and I realized I should stop trying to give it back."
—Mel White

counselors had characterized to him as an abomination worthy of execution and eternal damnation. Even as he penned bestsellers for Falwell and Robertson—albeit before their anti-gay rhetoric had taken center stage—White was popping Valium like candy and attending "ex-gay" ministries seeking a "cure" for his unwelcome feelings. At one point he visited a counselor who prescribed self-administered electroshock therapy. He tried exorcism. On three different occasions, White seriously considered suicide; once, he slashed his wrists open with the end of a coat hanger. For a man so blessed, he was terribly bedeviled.

Oliver North, Pat Robertson, Billy Graham, Jerry Falwell, and Newt Gingrich

WRESTLING WITH ANGELS

White had known he was romantically attracted to men from a very young age. And having been raised in a strict evangelical family, he also knew that his church frowned upon homosexuality. He kept his feelings to himself through school, and hoped that if he just worked harder, won more awards, scored more touchdowns, and was elected student body president, the "sin" and "defect" in his heart would be outweighed in the eyes of God.

As a young adult, he studied theology, became a preacher, and dedicated his life to witnessing for Jesus. He produced and starred in a Christian youth television program in Portland, produced evangelical films, and led dozens of Youth for Christ rallies around the Pacific Northwest. He married his best friend from high-school, Lyla, and settled down. He tried to ignore the gnawing feelings when he saw a handsome young man on the street or in a magazine.

Later in life, he imagined that perhaps another award for his filmmaking, or another bestselling book on the redemptive power of faith would cancel out his one secret "failing." But no matter how much he achieved—and he achieved much—he felt oppressive guilt, shame, and helplessness, and feared that he was disappointing his God, that God was on the verge of giving up on him.

Perhaps his meteoric career was a case of overcompensation. But never was White's faith shaken. "I knew God loved me. I never questioned that. And yet I wondered, if what the preachers and ministers said was true, how could God love me? It was that strange paradox many gay Christians feel; I knew God loved me, and at the same time I feared He didn't."

White was told throughout his life, as many gay Christians are, that if he prayed hard enough and believed deeply enough, he could overcome his homosexuality. He knows that the people who told him these things were, for the most part, well-meaning; they wanted to save his soul as much as he wanted to win souls to Christ through his films, books, local television shows, youth rallies, and ministries. But even so, the message had wounded him deeply, forced him to live a lie for 40 years, and nearly cost him his life.

DECLARATION OF WAR

Mel White reached his breaking point at about the same time the Christian right began seeking a new mission. It had long used fear to mobilize followers and raise funds, and until the late 1980s, Communism was a convenient target and in great supply overseas. But as the Communist bloc crumbled and the Berlin Wall fell, the evangelical movement in America needed new enemies. It chose abortion and homosexuality as its primary targets.

By the early 1990s, while White was working primarily as a speechwriter for Oliver North and the Rev. Billy Graham, the religious right declared war on homosexuality. America's postal system was soon overflowing with millions of solicitations from such evangelists as Falwell, Robertson, James Dobson of Focus on the Family, and Lou Sheldon of the Traditional Values Coalition, begging for donations to help fight the new scourge of the "homosexual agenda." In one appeal, Falwell wrote that gays "have a godless humanistic scheme for our nation—a plan which will destroy America's traditional moral values," and that gays and lesbians wanted the "complete elimination of God and Christianity from American society." Another Falwell solicitation letter asked his followers to sign a "Declaration of War" against the gay menace. A Traditional Values Coalition message claimed that a gay march on Washington had

ACT NOW   www.soulforce.org

been attended primarily by "militant and angry homosexuals demanding the right to sodomize 16-year-old boys." Callers to Christian right radio stations were suddenly calling for a wholesale round-up and slaughter of gays, and letters to newspapers claimed that AIDS was God's punishment for homosexuality.

Although White had never written anything anti-gay on behalf of any of his clients, he was feeling increasingly uncomfortable. For many years, he believed they were right about homosexuality, even as he knew he was gay. But things had suddenly changed; now his friends were openly at war with a part of him, a part that no matter how hard he tried, he was beginning to realize he could never change.

COMING TO THE TRUTH

In the early 1990s, White began taping Robertson's *700 Club* television program and collecting every piece of Christian-right mail he could. He began compiling an archive of the hate language being used against gays by his current and former employers. Simultaneously, he began tracking statistics of hate crimes against gays, and watched as the rates skyrocketed right along with the volume of hateful rhetoric. The time had come for him to take a stand.

"God gave me my sexuality as a gift, and I realized I should stop trying to give it back," says White. "My fears had kept me paralyzed for so long, that I felt like my life began right then. Once I had accepted it as a gift from God, I had to tell people. It would have been wrong to keep it a secret." White came out of the closet, first quietly in personal letters to Falwell and Graham in 1991 and 1992, and then publicly in 1993 when he was installed as Dean of the Cathedral of Hope in Dallas, the centerpiece of the Universal Fellowship of Metropolitan

Community Churches. UFMCC is the largest network of Christian churches ministering specifically to gays and lesbians. Before his first sermon, he spoke these words publicly for the first of many times to come: "I am gay. I am proud. And God loves me without reservation."

"To Jerry Falwell, Pat Robertson, and my other old clients on the religious right whose antigay rhetoric is killing us...I say this: I will not hate you, for Jesus said, 'Love your enemies.' I will not plot revenge against you, for Jesus said, 'Do good to those who despitefully use you and persecute you for my name's sake.' And I will not stoop to using your techniques: half-truths, hyperbole, and lies, for Jesus said, 'The truth shall set you free.'

"But this, too, I promise. I will not remain silent any longer. The religious right is wrong: wrong about the Bible, wrong about Jesus, wrong about God, wrong about the church, wrong about the family, and seriously wrong about gay and lesbian people. I pledge myself to do my best to prove you wrong with all the courage, wisdom, and love I can muster."

Falwell, Robertson, Graham, and all of White's other conservative Christian clients dropped him instantly, and cut off communication with him. He had gone from the ultimate insider to the most reviled outsider in the space of a single Sunday.

White was suddenly a cause celebre, the secretly gay pal of the anti-gay brigade. Within a week, he was on *Larry King Live, 60 Minutes,* and *The Today Show,* and in every major newspaper and magazine. When his autobiography came out later that summer, it shot up the *New York Times* bestseller list.

PREPARING FOR BATTLE

White says Falwell and Robertson and their ilk are "selective literalists" who deliberately misinterpret Bible passages to support their hateful ideas. White's mission in life now is to turn their hearts and make them understand and acknowledge that their words of intolerance destroy families and the lives of gay Christians, and implicitly condone and even incite violence against gay people.

White understood that he was in an incredibly good position to get their attention. After all, he had been friends with Falwell for a decade already, and the two played good-natured practical jokes on each other. "That's why I have hope for Jerry. He knows me, he knows I'm a good person. Now, he also knows I'm gay and he's going to have to figure out what to do with that."

First White looked to the Bible for guidance on how to approach the evangelists who were spouting the worst lies. In Matthew 18:15, Jesus had some advice for him on the matter: "If your brother sins against you, go and show him his fault, just between the two of you. If he listens to you, you have won your brother over. But if he will not listen, take one or two others along so that every matter may be established by the testimony of two or three witnesses. If he refuses to listen to them, tell it to the church; and if he refuses to listen even to the church, treat him as you would a pagan or a tax collector."

So in 1995, White sent a letter to Pat Robertson asking for a meeting to discuss Robertson's statements about homosexuality on the *700 Club*, and to talk about hate crimes against gays and lesbians. Robertson wrote back, refusing to meet with White, and accusing him of being "in league with the Devil." Not willing to give up, White invited a Unitarian minister and a rabbi—his witnesses—to come with him to the Virginia Beach headquarters of Robertson's Christian Broadcasting Network on Valentine's Day and try to speak with the evangelist. When they arrived, White was quickly arrested for trespassing and thrown in the local jail. Frustrated, he decided to fast until Robertson agreed to meet with him.

For three weeks, White ate nothing and survived only on water and the good wishes of supporters who sent truckloads of letters urging him on. The media swarmed around the jail and around Robertson's network headquarters. Finally, on the 21st night of White's fast Robertson appeared outside his cell, angry but beaten.

Calmly, White explained to Robertson that his vitriolic rhetoric was creating an atmosphere of violence that was contributing to the recent spike in hate crimes against gays and lesbians. White pleaded with Robertson to tone down the rhetoric and publicly condemn the violence. As soon as White was finished, Robertson turned and left. Moments later the sheriff opened White's cell and set him free. Although Robertson did make a public statement shortly afterward insisting that he did not condone violence against gays and lesbians, he emphasized again that he was opposed to homosexuality and believed God was, too.

Among friends later, White said he was "giving up" on Robertson. "That's an act of violence," said Lynn Cothran, who was then executive assistant to both Coretta Scott King and Maya Angelou. That day Cothran, a veteran of the American civil rights movement, became White's mentor on matters of nonviolence and civil disobedience.

LOVE THY ENEMY

Over the next few years, White dedicated himself full-time to studying Gandhi and Martin Luther King and their principles of nonviolence. He and his partner of 20 years, Gary Nixon, founded Soulforce, a nonprofit organization dedicated to teaching the principles of nonviolence to gay-rights activists and organizing against the religious right. In 1998, the American Civil Liberties Union awarded White the National Civil Liberties Award for his Soulforce efforts.

In 1999, White succeeded in convincing his old friend Jerry Falwell to help him stage an "anti-violence" summit in Falwell's hometown of Lynchburg, Virginia. In a lecture hall at Falwell's Liberty University, 200 Falwell supporters gathered with 200 gay Christians. By the end of it, Falwell had promised to choose his words more carefully and tone down his rhetoric. It was a short-lived victory: in September 2001 on Pat Robertson's *700 Club*, Falwell blamed abortion advocates and gays and lesbians for the terrorist attacks on America.

Gordon Robertson, son of Pat, hosts the 700 Club television show in Virginia Beach.

So in September of 2002, Mel White and Gary Nixon moved into a little house across the street from Falwell's Thomas Road Baptist church. They attend services every Sunday, take communion, and place generous checks in the offering plate. "Our presence there creates conflict for him. That's what direct action is all about!" says White. White and Nixon aren't leaving until Falwell listens. Really listens.

One of the principles White lives by, which he borrowed from Gandhi, is "Speak the truth in love relentlessly." And if White is anything, it is relentless. "Some might call it stubborn," he laughs.

While he holds out only the tiniest glimmer of hope that Falwell or Robertson will ever change their minds about homosexuality, White says he will never stop trying. "Every selfless act is a selfish act. This battle renews my spirit. I'm having fun. I am happier on the front lines than I would be behind a pulpit. When we are here, we are human."

Members of Soulforce protest the Southern Baptist convention in 2002.

❤ GET INVOLVED

Soulforce
PO Box 4467
Laguna Beach, CA 92652
Tel.: (949) 455-0999
Web site: www.soulforce.org
Email: info@soulforce.org

Universal Fellowship of Metropolitan Community Churches
8704 Santa Monica Blvd., 2nd Floor
West Hollywood, CA 90069-4548
Tel.: (310) 360-8640
Web site: www.mcchurch.org

Changing Attitude UK
A network of lesbian, gay, bisexual, and transgendered members of the four Anglican churches of the United Kingdom.
12 Lavender Gardens
Battersea, London, SW11 1DL
United Kingdom
Tel: 020 7738 1305
Fax: 020 7738 0584
Mobile: 07770 844302
Email: changinguk@freeuk.com
Web site: www.changingattitude.org

Dignity/USA
A Catholic organization supporting gay, lesbian, bisexual, and transgendered people of faith.
1500 Massachussetts Ave. NW
Suite #11
Washington, DC 20005-1894
United States
Tel.: (800) 877-8797
Email: dignity@aol.com
Web site: www.dignityusa.org

Affirmation
A worldwide organization for gay and lesbian Mormons.
P.O. Box 46022
Los Angeles, CA 90046-0022
United States
Tel.: (323) 255-7251
Web site: www.affirmation.org

Stranger at the Gate: To Be Gay and Christian in America
by Mel White
Plume/Penguin Books, 1993

THE SOULFORCE PRINCIPLES

Gandhi first used the term "soul force" to describe his principles of nonviolent resistance, or satyagraha. Martin Luther King later adopted the term and much of Gandhi's method for the American civil rights movement. Mel White has adapted both Gandhi and King's principles and methods for the gay-rights struggle. Among the directives:

Refuse to remain silent and inactive in the face of injustice.

Believe that God (the Universe, or Higher Power) is on the side of justice.

Believe that within everyone (even your worst adversary) there is an amazing potential for positive change.

See your adversary not as an evil person but as a victim of misinformation.

Try to win your adversary's friendship and understanding.

Speak the truth in love relentlessly (without half-truth, lie, or exaggeration), trying to persuade your adversary on the basis of truth alone.

Attack the false idea, not the person who holds the idea.

Believe that it is as much a moral obligation to refuse to cooperate with evil as it is to cooperate with good.

Insist that the means be as pure as the end.

Insist on nonviolence.

Avoid internal violence of the spirit (hate) as well as physical violence.

Accept and absorbing suffering without retaliation.

Do not fear death.

STAGES OF A SOULFORCE ACTION

Recommit yourself to the nonviolent soul force principles. Before you take on any untruth seriously, review the soul force principles. Recommit yourself and your allies to them. Sign a nonviolence pledge.

Research. Do not approach your opponent (the source of untruth) or the media until you have a carefully documented case. Details. Details. Details.

Negotiate. Take your case directly to your adversary. Try to settle the matter amicably, outside the public arena, but present the truth in love relentlessly.

Educate. If no reconciliation is reached, present your carefully documented case to the public through the media. Be sure everyone understands both the untruth and the truth involved. Continue to negotiate with your adversary.

Direct action/confrontation. If your adversary refuses to see the truth, escalate the conflict through direct nonviolent action. Present the truth in love relentlessly.

Reconciliation. Your goal is to bring your adversary to an understanding of the truth and create a world where you and your adversary can live in peace.

JOSE IGNACIO CABEZÓN

BUDDHIST GAY LIBERATIONIST

Jose Cabezon's spiritual path may be crooked, but he always seems to know where he's headed. He was born Catholic, but in early adulthood became a Buddhist monk. An eminent Buddhist scholar, these days Cabezon is a professor of religious studies at the University of California at Santa Barbara and a vocal advocate for gay rights and spiritual liberation. In an interview with *What Is Enlightenment?* magazine, Cabezon explained why he is an activist: "Someone who is committed to the Mahayana Buddhist path is committed to ending the suffering of others. One aspect of that is ending oppression and inequality wherever they exist. It seems to me that anyone who is seriously following the Mahayana Buddhist path would have to be committed to various forms of social liberation, including gay liberation, as a natural corollary of the Mahayana path, whether or not one is gay."

For many years, Cabezon worked as the Dalai Lama's translator, but eventually found himself at odds with the holy leader on the subject of homosexuality. In his book *Beyond Dogma*, the

Dalai Lama wrote that homosexuality is considered "misconduct" in Buddhist teachings. Cabezon wanted to calmly dispute the leader's interpretation. In 1997, a historic meeting between the supreme spiritual leader of Tibet and a handful of gay Buddhists and human rights activists took place in San Francisco, California.

Cabezon argued that when taken out of context, parts of some Buddhists texts can be interpreted to make a distinction between homosexual and heterosexual activity, but singling homosexuality out is not consistent with the Buddha's overall teaching.

For example, straight couples are permitted by the teachings to have sexual intercourse as many as five times in a row. Already, that seems in conflict with the ultimate Buddhist ideal to transcend desire. "Why are heterosexuals allowed sex up to five consecutive times and homosexuals zero?" Cabezon asked. The Dalai Lama laughed, "You have a point there!"

 # LEARN MORE

Gay Buddhist Fellowship
An organization advocating a gay-inclusive view of Buddhist teachings.
2215-R Market Street
San Francisco, CA 94114
United States
Tel.: (415) 974-9878
Web site: www.gaybuddhist.org

Queer Dharma:
Voices of Gay Buddhists (Vol. 1 & 2)
Winston Leyland, editor
Gay Sunshine Press, 1998 and 2002

BAYARD RUSTIN

QUAKER CIVIL-RIGHTS ORGANIZER

The 1963 March on Washington at which Martin Luther King gave his famous "I Have a Dream" speech might never have happened if it weren't for Bayard Rustin.

Dubbed "Mr. March" by his friend and fellow activist A. Philip Randolph, Rustin was the organizational brains behind many of King's biggest and most successful demonstrations, and one of King's foremost advisers on the tactics of nonviolent civil disobedience.

Rustin was naturally drawn to social justice movements. His grandmother Julia was among the earliest members of the National Association for the Advancement of Colored People (NAACP). Great civil rights leaders such as W.E.B. DuBois and Ida Wells often stopped in at the Rustin place on their way through Pennsylvania.

A Quaker by birth, Rustin refused a 1944 draft summons on the grounds that his Quaker beliefs forbade it. He spent the next two and a half years of his life in a federal penitentiary. When he was free again in 1947, Rustin helped organize "the Journey of Reconciliation," which became the first of the legendary "freedom rides." He was arrested for his part in the protest, and spent 30 days on a chain gang in North Carolina.

ACT NOW   www.rustin.org

"The major aspect of the struggle comes from without. If one gets out and begins to defend one's rights and the rights of others, spiritual growth takes place. One becomes in the process of doing, in the purifying process of action."

—Bayard Rustin

In 1955, Rustin helped King organize the bus boycott in Montgomery, Alabama, to protest segregation on that city's bus system. By the end of the boycott, Rustin was King's primary adviser. Together, they founded the Southern Christian Leadership Conference, a key civil-rights organization.

So why wasn't Rustin a celebrated folk hero? Probably because he was gay, and openly so, which was unusual for the time. On at least one occasion, he was arrested for homosexual behavior, which was then illegal in every state in America. He also had briefly belonged to the Communist party, and some in the civil rights movement thought those two facts combined made him an easy target for the right wing, which was eager to discredit King's growing movement.

Just before the March on Washington, an FBI agent hid in bushes outside King's bathroom window and shot a photo of the two men talking while King took a bath. The FBI then leaked the photo, along with a false rumor that Rustin and King were having a gay affair. Few believed it. King consistently leapt to Rustin's defense when others, suggested that Rustin was a weak link and should be removed from the inner circle.

In his later life, Rustin was active in liberation movements in colonial Africa, and in the struggle against apartheid in South Africa. He opposed the Vietnam war, and co-founded the A. Philip Randolph Foundation for black labor organizing. He took up the cause of gay rights in the 1980s, saying, "The barometer of where one is on human rights questions is no longer the black community, it's the gay community. Because it is the gay community which is most easily mistreated."

❤ LEARN MORE

The Bayard Rustin Fund
340 West 28th St., Suite 9J
New York, NY 10001
Tel.: (212) 242-5859

American Socrates: The Life of Bayard Rustin
A film in progress
Web site: www.rustin.org

Bayard Rustin: Troubles I've Seen:
A Biography
by Jervis Anderson
University of California Press, 1998

Bayard Rustin and the Civil Rights Movement
by Daniel Levine
Rutgers University Press, 1999

Bayard Rustin: Behind the Scenes in the Civil
Rights Movement
by James Haskins
Hyperion Press, 1997

♥ GET INVOLVED

These organizations work on behalf of gay and lesbians of all races and religous affiliations.

Gay and Lesbian Alliance Against Defamation
248 West 35th Street, 8th Floor
New York, NY 10001
Tel.: (212) 629-3322
Web site: www.glaad.org

National Gay & Lesbian Task Force
1325 Massachusetts Ave. NW, Suite 600
Washington, D.C. 20005
Tel.: (202) 393-5177
Email: ngltf@ngltf.org
Web site: www.ngltf.org

Human Rights Campaign
919 18th St. NW, Suite 800
Washington, D.C. 20006
Tel.: (202) 628-4160
Web site: www.hrc.org

International Gay and Lesbian Human Rights Commission
1375 Sutter Street, Suite 222
San Francisco, CA 94109
United States
Tel.: (415) 561-0633
Web site: www.iglhrc.org

Equality Alliance UK
PO Box 637
Dagenham, Essex
RM10 7GG
United Kingdom
Web site: www.equalityalliance.org.uk

South African Lesbian and Gay Equality Project
PO Box 27811, Yeoville
Johannesburg, 2143
South Africa
Tel.: 27 + 11 487-3810
Email: info@equality.org.za
Web site: www.equality.org.za

SHALOM, SALAM

NETA GOLAN

BUDDHIST JEW, MIDDLE EAST PEACE ACTIVIST

I n the summer of 2002, Neta Golan sneaked into both the besieged compound of Palestinian leader Yasser Arafat and the Church of the Nativity where dozens of Palestinians were holed up against mortar fire from the Israeli army. Before she and a handful of activists from around the world arrived, Arafat's compound had been shelled twice, and three Palestinians inside had been killed.

After she arrived, the shelling stopped. Neta Golan, an Israeli Jew, believes she and her fellow activists created an impossible situation for the Israeli government—to kill Arafat, or even one more Palestinian inside the compound, would risk killing Israelis and international observers. The only hope for resolution from that moment became negotiation. "It was dangerous, and we were scared, of course we were scared," says Golan. "But it worked."

It's all in a day's work for Golan, who has repeatedly and voluntarily put herself bodily between Palestinian civilians and Israeli settlers and soldiers in an effort to stop the violence from both sides. She has lain down in front of Israeli Defense Force (IDF) tanks headed to demolish Palestinian villages; she has been shot at by Jewish settlers in the West Bank; she has had her arm broken by Israeli police after organizing a nonviolent protest and vigil at the site of a new and illegal Jewish settlement in Palestinian territory.

As co-founder of the International Solidarity Movement (ISM), Golan is now training Palestinians, Israelis, and international activists in the principles of nonviolence in the hopes that the struggle for Palestinian liberation will not be decided by the volume of blood flowing in the streets.

A HUMAN DETERRENT

Plenty of people think she's crazy; she has difficulty countering the observation that she is perhaps, at least passively, suicidal. But she says she has a moral responsibility to do what she can to stop the violence and to advance the cause of the Palestinians, who she believes have been oppressed and subjugated by a racist and entrenched Israeli establishment for far too long. And so, wherever the Israeli army is preparing to bulldoze a refugee camp, Golan and her ISM cohorts stand between the earthmovers and the refugees. Wherever Jewish

International peace activists enter Manger Square against Israeli Army orders in 2002.

settlers are shooting into Palestinian villages, Golan stands in the line of fire, daring them to kill her. These days, the Israeli army has adopted a policy of bombing or bulldozing the homes of suicide bombers. So Golan and ISM activists from around the world are moving into those houses before the tanks get there. If the IDF insists on demolishing the house, they will have to do so with Israeli, Canadian, European, and Japanese civilians inside.

Truly a movement rather than a political party or organization, the ISM is a loose, interfaith network with chapters in a half-dozen countries, including Denmark, Japan, Sweden, Italy, and the United Kingdom. Volunteers are asked to come to Palestine for 30 days before they put themselves in harm's way. The ISM carefully trains every volunteer in five basic areas:

1. The principles and tactics of nonviolent civil disobedience

2. Protestors' legal rights should they be injured or arrested

3. How to handle the media

4. The historical context of the region, including both Israeli and Palestinian claims to the land

5. Cultural considerations for working with and living among Palestinians

Some chapters train volunteers in conflict resolution and negotiation techniques, basic Arabic, and first aid, as well. Every volunteer is warned of the danger of participation. "You may be arrested, you may be deported, you may be injured, you may be killed. It has all happened before, and it is real," says Golan. "We tell everybody so they know what is at stake."

EYES WIDE OPEN

Golan was not raised in a strictly religious household (though her mother embraced Orthodox Judaism when Neta was in her teens), but she attended Jewish schools, where Jewish history and religion were taught as regularly as arithmetic. "We were simply taught the Jewish history of oppression and dispossession over and over again," she says. "In school, the Jews were always portrayed as the victim; even the establishment of Israel, in this context, was presented as an act of self-defense."

Back then, Israelis didn't even refer to "Palestinians," because that would imply they had some claim to Palestine. There were only Israelis and Arabs. "The occupation was simply not discussed," Golan says. "It was a taboo subject. The ethnic cleansing of Palestinians in 1948, and the ongoing subjugation of Palestinians under the occupation was invisible to the mostly secular Israeli people." Including Golan.

"I was taught that Arabs were inherently violent, that they did not understand ethics, and that they all wanted to kill me simply because I was Jewish. This is all I heard. It didn't occur to me to question it because I was never told that there was another side to the story. It was pure racism presented as fact."

Golan was 15 years old when a woman spoke to her class about human rights. On that fateful day, Golan's life was changed and her view of her homeland shattered.

"She told us about people being arrested without being charged, disappearing for weeks at a time without explanation, about people who were not legally permitted to gather together in

ACT NOW www.palsolidarity.org

A Palestinian mother mourns for her two children who were killed when Israeli soldiers bombed a refugee camp in the Gaza Strip.

their own villages, who were persecuted and tortured and living in basically prison conditions in their own homes," Golan recalls. "I remember thinking, 'You're talking about Argentina! Certainly not Israel!'"

But the woman *was* speaking of Israel. And Golan felt the first pull toward her now famous solidarity with the Palestinian people. In the years that followed, Golan dodged the Israeli draft, fled to Canada, and discovered Buddhism. She studied the principles of Buddhist meditation, and began her self-prescribed education in spiritual nonviolent resistance.

She met Thich Nhat Hanh, and spent several months at his Plum Village Buddhist retreat in France. Later she traveled to India to practice meditation in prolonged silence. She calls her education in the history and practice of spiritual nonviolence spotty and inelegant, but it was enough to motivate her to return home and put these new ideas and ideals into action.

She says she was not shocked by the outbreak of the second Intifada in 2000, because she had already been living in the West Bank for several years with her Palestinian husband. She had seen the tensions building; it was only a matter of when the anger would explode. But Golan was shocked at the brutality of the Israeli response, and especially the tacit complicity of the international community. Finally, she had to do something.

EXTENDING THE OLIVE BRANCH

In 2000, Golan heard of growing tensions around the Palestinian village of Hares. The town is ringed by centuries-old olive orchards. As in many Palestinian communities, the olive crop is the core of the village's traditional livelihood. But after the beginning of the second Intifada, the Israeli army began bulldozing the olive orchards, blocking the town from all remaining trees, and cutting it off from the main road with huge earthen berms.

Since the beginning of the Intifada, 200,000 olive trees in Palestine have been uprooted by Israeli soldiers and settlers, at an economic cost to Palestinians of more than $10 million dollars. In Hares, the villagers' connection to the land and tradition demanded they try to maintain what they could of the old ways. They had to harvest. Without easy access to the orchards, the Hares villagers were faced with the loss of their crop, and even more desperate economic times. The fruit ripened on the branches, but within weeks, would wither and rot.

Desperate and determined villagers clambered over the earthen berms and tried to harvest the olives. But they were met with rifle fire from the neighboring Jewish religious colony of

Ravava. Palestinian youths tried to fend off the settlers with stones, provoking the Israeli army to step in and threaten deadly force.

One morning, Neta Golan walked out into the middle of the main road between Ravava and Hares. On one side were about 40 Jewish settlers with rifles. On the other, about 100 unarmed Palestinians. Off in the distance, but close enough to see and hear, stood Israeli soldiers.

As Golan explained in Hebrew over a loudspeaker that the Hares villagers simply wanted to remove the roadblock and gain access to their orchards, the settlers spit out hateful remarks and threats of rape in response. Golan reminded them that she was an Israeli Jew, and if they opened fire on the village as they had in the past (killing one teenage boy and injuring dozens of unarmed civilians), they would kill her first. Impasse.

The standoff stretched on, the villagers behind Golan successfully removed the roadblock. Tempers on the settler side flared. As night fell, the settlers gathered with rifles and marched toward the roadblock and Golan. The Israeli soldiers did nothing. Moments later a shot rang out. The bullet hit so close to Golan, a shard of rock from the road flew up and buried itself in her cheek.

On the loudspeaker, the bleeding Golan addressed the Israeli soldiers, who had violated military law by not intervening when the settlers advanced. "We have cameras here, and can document this attack. I will lodge a complaint with the military courts that you stood by and did nothing, which is a crime. You will go to the stockade." Reluctantly, the soldiers moved in

and dispersed the settlers. Within weeks, the roadblock was back. And so was Golan, and then other international observers and Israelis sympathetic to her efforts. The mayor of Hares later told *The London Times* that Golan "has saved lives and brought us hope that the Israelis might be able to live with us in peace one day."

THE ROOTS OF RESISTANCE

Golan says the fact she's a Jew with a deep sense of her own people's oppression and dispossession makes her especially compassionate to the Palestinian predicament. "Being a Jew for me is not a matter of religion and being Israeli is not a matter of ideology but those are my roots. That is the culture I was brought up with and conditioned in," she explains. "Jews have a history of struggling for justice, which I feel I have inherited...growing up, the Holocaust was always my reference point."

The unhealed pain from that collective trauma is keeping some people from being open to the pain of other people."

Golan rejects charges from her critics, particularly among the Israeli right-wing, that she is a "self-hating Jew" because she so passionately defends the Palestinians. She says it's precisely the opposite: Her deep sense of her own Jewishness compels her to activism on the part of the Palestinians. "If you are not careful, you become what you hate. Many Jews hate the Nazis and believe that we could never, would never under any circumstances, be capable of such atrocities. Such denial of our potential as humans to act inhumanly is dangerous, because we do not recognize these qualities when they arise in us.

"The wound that I carry from the Holocaust is most of the world's apathy while the atrocities where being committed. As a Jew of East European descent, I am committed to not being apathetic towards others who are suffering from racial discrimination and violence and doing what I can to stand with them.

"There is a mainstream commitment in Israel that we should do everything in our power to prevent another Holocaust from happening...*to us*. I am part of a minority that is working so that the Holocaust never happens again, *period*."

Golan admits to struggling with her dedication to nonviolence. She recalls Thich Nhat Hanh himself talking about the Buddhist precept that dictates an inviolable reverence for all life and forbids one from condoning killing of any kind for any reason. That sort or moral absolutism can be difficult, Golan says, when you see Palestinians so desperate, and the retaliation by the Israelis so lethal and excessive. She says that while she does not condone violence such as suicide bombings or even rock-throwing, she can certainly understand where it comes from. "When you push a people way beyond a boiling point—like when you put a cat in the corner and attack it—you know it's going to attack," she told *The Jerusalem Post*. Golan attributes the increased militancy of the most recent Intifada to the practical failure of the "peace process," which resulted in many promises to Palestinians that were never fulfilled. "When popular resistance, in this case the mostly unarmed first Intifada, is suppressed, a more militant force emerges."

Still, nonviolence is a two-way street, and the integrity of Golan's ISM depends on her not making excuses for Palestinian violence, either. "When I am feeling particularly angry or hurt or helpless, it is easy to emotionally justify violence. There is a danger of being overcome with grief and hate. But I have to keep reminding myself: When we demonstrate out of a pure sense of love rather than revenge, it can only benefit both sides. The more humanity you bring to a situation, the better it will be. We are delivering compassion and love into situations where they are hard to find."

Now, when Golan is invited to lead a nonviolent protest in a Palestinian village, she makes clear one central and absolute condition: If Palestinians throw rocks, the ISM volunteers will leave, making the village vulnerable to attack. "They have a choice. They can demonstrate nonviolently and we will be there to support and defend them. If they choose to throw stones, we will leave." The condition is usually agreed upon.

"It is not my job to tell Palestinians how to resist, but I believe it is my job to provide an alternative. Already most Palestinians are resisting nonviolently; they are removing roadblocks

ACT NOW   www.palsolidarity.org

and going around checkpoints and harvesting their olives, and for all of these things they are shot at. Yet they go on just trying to live decent, dignified lives. We are just trying to give these people a chance to resist peacefully without dying."

But Golan knows that the more she stands between armed combatants with centuries-old animosities, the more she tempts her own fate. She relies on her Buddhist faith and practice to stay sane. "It is my strength," she says. "I have learned not to react with hurt or anger, but with respect and compassion. It has become a habit for me to approach soldiers, to approach the war machine that is aggressive by nature, with compassion. Because it fucks it up; it isn't built for love, and it doesn't know what to do with it. Each soldier is really hungry for the opportunity to show their humanity, so I give it to them. And it works."

Although she willingly puts herself in harm's way, she has no aspirations for martyrdom. There is a difference, she says, between a principled willingness to die for a cause and an extremist's hunger for martyrdom. "Martin Luther King said the only life worth living is one you're willing to give up for what you believe. You have to be willing to sacrifice your life for a better future. It's not something to aspire to, but it is something I have to accept. That's my choice: I prefer to be killed than to be violent."

💗 GET INVOLVED

International Solidarity Movement
An international interfaith organization co-founded by Neta Golan that trains international activists to use nonviolent direct action to resist Israeli occupation forces and policies.
Email: info@palsolidarity.org
Web site: www.palsolidarity.org or www.directactionpalestine.com

Gush Shalom (Israeli Peace Bloc)
Founded by the activist and journalist Uri Avnery, Gush Shalom is the "hard core" of the Israeli peace movement dedicated to ending the violence and to establishment of two states—Israel and Palestine—with Jerusalem as their shared capital.
PO Box 3322
Tel-Aviv 61033 Israel
Email: info@guah-shalom.org
Web site: www.gush-shalom.org

Peace Now
Founded in 1978 by 348 reserve officers and soldiers of the Israel Defense Forces, Peace Now calls itself a Zionist organization that believes that "a democratic, Jewish state can and must be secured without subjugating another people." It is a nonpartisan volunteer movement with branches throughout Israel, in the major cities and in the kibbutz movement.
Email: info@peacenow.org.il
Web site: www.peacenow.org.il

Rabbis for Human Rights
An Israeli rabbinic organization comprising Reform, Orthodox, Conservative, and Reconstructionist rabbis and students dedicated to "giving voice to the Jewish tradition of human rights."
Yitzhak Elhanan 2,
Jerusalem 92141 Israel
Tel.: 972-2-563-7731
Email: info@rhr.israel.netz
Web site: http://rhr.israel.net

JEAN ZARU

QUAKER PALESTINIAN PEACE ADVOCATE

Advancing the cause of nonviolence in the Israeli-occupied territories is a Sisyphian challenge. So it is fortunate that such a task has fallen to a woman who is undeterred by the odds. Jean Zaru is a rare breed indeed: a Palestinian Arab who also happens to be a Quaker in an overwhelmingly Jewish and Muslim land. A minority among a persecuted minority, Zaru has taken it upon herself to assemble a vocal and visible group of Palestinians and Israelis—Jews, Muslims, and Christians alike—to speak out against violence on both sides of the seemingly intractable conflict in the Middle East.

Zaru was born in Ramallah to Quaker parents. She was 8 years old when the war of 1948 broke out and refugee family members from surrounding towns came to live in the family's three-room apartment. In 1967, her husband—the principal at the Ramallah Friends School where Zaru taught—was badly injured when Israeli gunships bombed the town. Her brother, a graduate of Harvard University, disappeared in Lebanon in the 1980s.

Zaru has lived most of her life under Israeli occupation, required to carry identification papers with her in order to pass though multiple checkpoints on her way to and from work and religious meetings. Part of Zaru's ministry is to tell her story and those of other Palestinians who have managed to maintain hope and dignity in the face of such suffering. She says that the Western media have failed to tell the truth about Palestinians' plight, and it is the

ACT NOW   www.sabeel.org

responsibility of every peace-loving Palestinian to fight to be heard. "My life experience is rooted in my identity as a Palestinian Quaker woman struggling to find a way of transformation in our broken world. Without a doubt, the way of transformation calls us to stand face to face with the forces of death and evil, both within us and around us," she said in a recent speech.

"The real turning point in the liberation experience is the public voicing of pain that is often and intentional, a communal act of expressing grievance. The act of crying out...is at once an act of subversion and an act of hope." The Israeli occupation is a form of "structural violence" according to Zaru, and is a bald provocation of the Palestinian people.

And although Zaru can commiserate with the frustration and grief of Palestinians who have suffered under brutal conditions for over half a century, she insists that violence against Israel and Israelis is not the answer.

"I admit, some Palestinians,

An Israeli soldier guards Palestinian men who came too close to a Jewish settlement.

in their anger and despair, have resorted to violence," Zaru said at a Quaker meeting in Philadelphia in 2002. "I, personally, do not think that violence can lead us anywhere, neither morally nor strategically."

"The victims of oppression are not always blameless," she said. "Far too often they become the oppressors of others. The way of Jesus takes radical Christianity back to the Gospel story of nonviolent protest and the implementation of the reign of God on earth. To resort to violence as an instrument of change is rejected as a strategy by Jesus."

❤ LEARN MORE

Sabeel Ecumenical Liberation Theology Center
Founded by Jean Zaru, this ecumenical pacifist group is modeled on the tradition of liberation theology.
PO Box 49084
Jerusalem 91491 Israel
Tel. (Israel): 972-2-532-7136
Tel. (U.S.): (971) 544-1313
Email: sabeel@sabeel.org
Web site: www.sabeel.org

American Friends Service Committee
Middle East Peacebuilding Program
1501 Cherry Street
Philadelphia, PA 19102
United States
Tel.: (215) 241-7019
Email: kbergen@afsc.org
Web site: www.afsc.org/mideasthome.htm

THICH NHAT HANH

BUDDHIST MONK, PEACE WORKER

To the reporters gathered on that Chicago summer day in 1966, they must have seemed an unlikely pair—the Zen Buddhist monk from central Vietnam standing alongside America's greatest apostle of racial equality and nonviolent protest. Thich Nhat Hanh and Martin Luther King Jr. had met for the first time just half an hour before. Their conversation had been so fruitful that they held a press conference on the spot, eager to convey their common opposition to the war that would devastate Vietnam and sear America's slumbering conscience.

A former professor at Columbia University and, before that, a student at Princeton, Hanh was by the mid-1960s known for founding the School of Youth for Social Services (SYSS) in Saigon. The grassroots relief organization, basing its work on the Buddhist principles of nonviolence and compassionate action, rebuilt bombed villages—some of them repeatedly—set up schools, medical centers, and agricultural cooperatives, and helped resettle the many families left homeless by the war. Over the years, SYSS grew to include more than 10,000 monks, nuns, and volunteers.

Before he was driven into exile, Hanh also established a peace-activist magazine; a publishing house, La Boi Press; and a Buddhist study center, the An Quang Pagoda—all in the face of government opposition.

ACT NOW www.plumvillage.org

Hanh had pushed the Buddhist Church in Vietnam to lead a nonviolent revolution to stop the war and unite North and South. "Our principle," he said, "is to come to poor people with our love, our care, our understanding, and make the revolution from what we have in our hand, in our ability." The church, considering him an idle dreamer, initially refused to help him, but was eventually won over by his teaching of "engaged Buddhism," combining traditional meditative practices and active non-violent civil disobedience. In 1969, Thich Nhat Hanh led the Vietnamese Buddhist peace delegation to the Paris peace talks, and remained until the signing of peace accords in 1973.

As for Dr. King, a year after their first meeting, King wrote these words to the Nobel Prize Committee: "As the Nobel Peace Prize Laureate of 1964, I now have the pleasure of proposing to you the name of Thich Nhat Hanh for that award in 1967. I do not personally know of anyone more worthy of the Nobel Peace Prize than this gentle Buddhist monk from Vietnam."

Hanh—still considered a threat by the Vietnamese government—has not been allowed to return home. He now resides in France, and in 1982 he founded Plum Village, a meditation community in the Bordeaux region of France, where he continues to teach, write, and garden.

❤ LEARN MORE

Plum Village
Le Pey 24240
Thenac, France
Tel.: +(33) 5 53 58 48 58
Fax: +(33) 5 53 57 34 43
Email: UH-office@plumvillage.org
Web site: www.plumvillage.org

Love in Action: Writings on Nonviolent Social Change
by Thich Nhat Hanh
Parallax Press, 1993

Peace is Every Step: The Path of Mindfulness in Everyday Life
by Thich Nhat Hanh
Bantam Books, 1992

The Heart of the Buddha's Teaching: Transforming Suffering into Peace, Joy & Liberation
by Thich Nhat Hanh
Broadway Books, 1999

Being Peace
by Thich Nhat Hanh
Parallax Press, 1996

MEENA KESHWAR KAMAL

MUSLIM FOUNDER, REVOLUTIONARY ASSOCIATION OF THE WOMEN OF AFGHANISTAN

Meena Keshwar Kamal founded the Revolutionary Association of the Women of Afghanistan in 1977. At the time, the Afghanistan government was deeply Islamic (as were Meena and most other Afghans), but compared to the fundamentalist regimes that would follow, Afghanistan in the mid-1970s was a relatively liberal place. Still, Meena and members of RAWA pushed for more secure rights for women, including the right to vote, equal access to quality health care, and a guaranteed right to education.

In 1978, a fundamentalist revolution swept the country, ousting the moderate leadership and replacing it with Muslim fundamentalists who established the brutal force of holy warriors known as the Mujahideen. Women were instantly stripped of their rights.

Less than a year later the Soviet Union invaded, and brutally subjugated all Afghanis, not just the leadership. Meena, opposed to the extremists on both sides of the Soviet-Afghan conflict yet caught between them, fled to neighboring Pakistan.

The work of RAWA quickly moved from protest rallies to humanitarian aid in Afghan refugee camps over the border in Pakistan. Meena set up a hospital and several mobile medical clinics to deliver health care to women and children in the camps. She also built schools for homeless Afghan children, and developed literacy and mathematics courses for Afghan women. She traveled the world, speaking of the horrible conditions in the camps and the destitution faced by Afghan women suddenly disenfranchised and persecuted by both Soviet invaders and radical fundamentalists.

In 1987, Meena was found assassinated along with two members of her family in her home in Quetta, Pakistan. No one took credit for the murders, so there are only theories about her killers. Some say it was the KGB, others say it was Islamic fundamentalist groups based in Pakistan, a few say it was both.

RAWA continues its work in refugee camps in Pakistan, and has opposed every fundamentalist regime in Afghanistan up to and including the Taleban. Islam, they insist, does not require the oppression of women, and the radical factions who have used religion to persecute women are not true Muslims. The group is now concentrating on reestablishing democracy and constitutionally guaranteed rights for women under the new Afghanistan leadership.

ACT NOW   www.rawa.org

❤ LEARN MORE

Revolutionary Association of Women of Afghanistan
The organization founded by Meena and still dedicated to the cause of women's rights in Afghanistan. It is a decentralized organization with no official headquarters or leader.
Web site: www.rawa.org

Afghan Women's Mission
The American wing of RAWA, the Afghan Women's Mission helps funnel donations and other resources to the disparate active members of RAWA in Afghanistan and Pakistan.
260 S. Lake Avenue
PO Box 165
Pasadena, CA 91101
Tel.: (509) 756-2236
Email: info@afghanwomensmission.org
Web site: www.afghanwomensmission.org

Veiled Courage: Inside the Afghan Women's Resistance
by Cheryl Benard and Edith Schlaffer
Broadway Books, 2002

Unveiled: Voices of Women in Afghanistan
by Harriet Logan
Regan Books, 2002

Price of Honor: Muslim Women Lift the Veil of Silence on the Islamic World
by Jan Goodwin
Little Brown & Company, 1994

Faith and Freedom: Women's Human Rights in the Muslim World
Mahnaz Afkhami, editor
Syracuse University Press, 1995

Qur'an and Woman: Rereading the Sacred Text from a Woman's Perspective
by Amina Wadud-Muhsin
Oxford University Press, 1999

HOPE AND

RESISTANCE

JANUSZ KORCZAK

JEWISH CHILD ADVOCATE

Head held high, an avuncular figure strode through the streets of the Warsaw Ghetto on a summer day in 1942. He did his best to provide a smile and words of reassurance for the 200 children who had grown to love and trust him, and whom he was now forced to betray.

Janusz Korczak was a much-admired children's book author, educator, child advocate, and pediatrician, as well as the administrator of a famous, progressive orphanage for the mostly Jewish street children of Warsaw. But he had been ordered by the Nazis to evacuate his orphanage and lead the children to a waiting train—a train the SS said would take the children to "resettlement in the east."

Korczak had known the Nazis would come for the children, and for him. His many non-Jewish friends, colleagues, and admirers showered him with offers of help in escaping to freedom. But he refused. "You do not leave a sick child in the night, and you do not leave children at a time like this," he reportedly said.

In order to chase away the children's terrors in those last horrible hours, Korczak and his assistant dressed all 200 in their smartest clothes and handed them their favorite toy or book for the trip. Then, at their side, he marched through the streets carrying the orphanage's flag,

ACT NOW www.korczak.com

"Behave decently, and do good. Pray, not to ask things of God, but so as not to forget Him, because one should see Him everywhere."
—Janusz Korczak

one side green decorated with white blossoms, the other side proudly bearing a Star of David. Eyewitness accounts say the children marched four across through the dirty streets of the Warsaw Ghetto, cheerfully singing in unison. Korczak boarded the cattle car with them, still singing. In all likelihood, they were all dead within days.

MORAL COMPASS

Born Henryk Goldszmit in Warsaw on July 22, 1879, Janusz Korczak (a pen name he adopted when he was 20) was the descendent of two generations of educated Jews who flourished among the liberal intelligentsia of pre-war Poland's multi-cultural society. His grandfather and namesake had been an early adherent of the Haskalah, or "Jewish Enlightenment Movement," which encouraged the Jewish diaspora to assimilate into secular society.

The Goldszmits considered themselves equally Polish and Jewish—a rare thing indeed in a society where Jews often lived separate from the gentile population by choice. The family spoke Polish instead of Hebrew, dressed in secular clothing, and worked in white-collar professions such as law, medicine, and journalism. They came under fire from both the anti-Semitic pockets of Polish society and from Jews who thought them traitors to their faith and culture. Living in this purgatory all his life shaped both Korczak's intellect and his seemingly boundless compassion.

Despite growing up in a loving and supportive household with all of his needs more than met, Korczak's childhood was not without tragedy. His father—a lawyer, publisher, and Talmudic scholar—was institutionalized when Korczak was just 11, and dead by Korczak's 18th birthday, probably of a progressive and hereditary neurological disease such as Huntington's chorea. But Korczak feared that it was syphilis, and worried that his own sexual longings—which ran to the homosexual—would doom him to a similar fate.

Korczak's adolescent angst drove him to write incessantly, from poems and fanciful novels to copious scribblings in his journals, which would later become the raw material for vaguely autobiographical works of fiction. He won a prestigious literary prize at age 20, but rejected writing as a career in itself. "Writing," he explained in his journal at the time, "is only words, while medicine is deeds."

As a young student, he had noticed how children in Polish society were regarded as property, often harshly punished and rarely praised. As the industrial revolution swept through eastern Europe and Russian troops continued their ruthless occupation of Poland, homelessness and poverty exploded, leaving hundreds of children shivering in the shadows. Although Korczak himself was well enough off, some of his earliest journal entries express a deep moral anguish at the plight of these street urchins, the first signs of his later celebrated preternatural empathy for young people.

CHILDREN FIRST

As a medical student at Warsaw University, he moved to a district stricken with poverty and widespread illiteracy. His friends were literary superstars, sympathetic to the revolutionary socialist rumblings in the industrializing cities. In his final years of study, he wrote the semi-autobiographical novel *Children of the Drawing Room*, which depicted the desperation of street children in Warsaw and brought him to national renown.

Despite his fame, he refused to give up medicine for a life in the rarefied circles of the literati. His affection for children still moved him to tutor them in his spare time, sometimes going into the darkest corners of the slums, under bridges, and in ditches along highways, to bring candy, medicine, and books to the children.

He graduated from the university in 1905 as a pediatrician, but was soon after conscripted by the Czar's army to serve in the Russian-Japanese war on a hospital train. The misery of the war zone shocked and angered Korczak, who was naturally drawn to the sides of suffering children. When a railway strike threatened the war effort, Korczak was ordered by his superiors to address the workers on behalf of the army. Instead of ordering the strikers back to work, he turned to the military delegation and said merely, "Before you go to war for any purpose you should stop to think of the innocent children who will be injured, killed, or orphaned."

When he returned from the war, Korczak the famous author, a veteran, a doctor, and a socialite, wouldn't accept a well-paid job in exclusive medical practices or hospitals. Instead, he took a job at the Warsaw Children's Hospital, which treated children of all faiths at low or no cost. He also began an academic life as a researcher and educator of medical students.

Over the following years, Korczak's reputation among medical experts and educators grew exponentially, mostly as the result of his uniquely empathic approach to the treatment of children. A student of his recalled a lecture Korczak delivered at the Institute of Pedagogy early in his career. He had arranged with a nearby orphanage to borrow a 4-year-old boy as a demonstration subject.

He wired the boy to monitors, and threw the switch on a massive X-ray machine, which roared to life. But Korczak had no intention of taking the boy's X-ray. The moment the assembled students saw the boy's heart rate leap wildly, the lesson was over. "Don't ever forget this sight," he told them. "How wildly a child's heart beats when he is frightened. And this it does even more so when reacting to an adult's anger with him, not to mention when he fears being punished." Heading for the door with the boy's hand in his, he added, "That is all for today."

Korczak continued writing throughout his career as doctor, educator, and child advocate. He published dozens of books on child development and education, and formulated his own list of the fundamental human rights to dignity and respect due all children, regardless of nationality or religious affiliation. His books *A Child's Right to Respect*, and *How to Love a Child*, have become classics of early childhood development education in Europe.

On his periodic sabbaticals from the hospital, Korczak organized summer camps in the countryside for Jewish street children. His volunteer work away from the dirty city became his greatest passion, especially as anti-Russian tensions mounted in Warsaw and Czarist oppression was leading ever more liberal intellectuals to be arrested and jailed. Korczak was himself vulnerable both for his Jewishness and for his repute as a liberal author and scholar, but still he did not worry about his own fate.

To him, the orphaned street children he encountered each day were the most urgent cause. He roamed the streets looking into their sunken eyes, and described them in a journal as "rare children who bear not only the weight of their 10 years, but deep in their souls the burden of many generations."

In 1909, Korczak was rounded up with other noted Jewish socialist intellectuals and thrown in jail by occupying Russian forces. Only the intervention of a well-placed Polish Gentile family whose child he had treated won Korczak's release. The experience jolted him. He announced that he was giving up both his medical and writing careers to help run a new Jewish orphanage in Warsaw, where he could put his philosophy about children into direct practice.

"The reason I became an educator was that I always felt best when I was among children," he said. Most of his friends, colleagues, and admirers were shocked that he would give up so much for such a seemingly modest new job. Korczak later explained: "The road I have chosen toward my goal is neither the shortest nor the most convenient. But it is the best for me because it is my own. I found it not without effort or pain, and only when I had come to understand that all the books I read, and all the experiences and opinions of others, were misleading."

ACT NOW www.korczak.com

A Polish boy returns to the ruins of his bombed home in Warsaw in 1943

A REVOLUTIONARY OF A DIFFERENT STRIPE

Korczak personally designed and planned the building in which the orphanage was to be housed. His design was innovative and visionary, conceived not only to keep the children in and provide the basic necessities, but to develop the orphans' mental, moral, and emotional well-being. Later, he founded a second orphanage, this one for Catholic children, across town. Korczak was about to revolutionize the concept of orphanages, which had been until then little more than warehouses for unwanted children.

Korczak himself would never marry or have children of his own. He considered his work a spiritual calling, of a seriousness that excluded his own desires, and took "a vow to uphold the child and defend his rights." As Betty Jean Lifton wrote in *The King of Children: The Life and Death of Janusz Korczak* (Pan Books, 1989), "No religious order had asked him for such a vow—but he was to uphold it as conscientiously as any priest."

Inside the orphanage, he attempted to create a self-governing "little republic" in which children helped to establish rules and were disciplined by tribunals of their own peers. Korczak helped them produce a newspaper by and about children, which was distributed around the country. Each had a responsibility to contribute to the smooth running of the entire communal household that was, in its self-contained way, a community, a school, a home, and a workplace for the children and educators alike. Korczak himself lived in the attic of the orphanage from the day it opened until the day he boarded the train to Treblinka.

Even as the orphanage experiment commanded the attention and admiration of educators around Europe, Korczak was feeling squeezed by the social tensions growing from either side.

Under the Russian occupation, anti-Semitism was exploding at the same time Polish nationalism was peaking. Polish Jews and Gentiles were mixing with less and less frequency, even among the intelligentsia. He still considered himself both a Jew and a Pole, and did not see this as any contradiction: "If anyone speaks Polish, desires the well-being of the Polish people, wishes them well, then he is also a Pole," he wrote in his diaries. Korczak began writing articles in prominent journals arguing that Poland could be both strong and proud, and tolerant of its Jewish population, even if Jews and gentiles chose to live separately.

In one such article, he wrote: "We are sons of the same clay. Ages of mutual suffering and success link us on the same chain, The same sun shines upon us, the same hail destroys our fields, the same earth hides the bones of our ancestors. There have been more tears than smiles in our history, but that was neither of our faults. Let us light a common fire together."

TORN BETWEEN TWO IDENTITIES

The end of World War I, in which Korczak was conscripted by the Russian forces as a medic, saw Poland reunited as an independent nation. But still Korczak was aware that his ethnicity and his nationality were at odds. His spirituality, albeit unconventional (he once wrote a collection of improvised prayers called *Alone with God: Prayers for Those Who Don't Pray*), provided his bridge. In her biography of Korczak, Betty Jean Lifton writes, "He had never been an observant Jew, but he had always been a man of faith. The God that Korczak believed in, like Spinoza's, was a free spirit, a mystical force that flowed through the universe." Korczak wrote once that, "It does not surprise me that God has no beginning and no end, because I see Him as unending Harmony. The stars, the very universe, inform me about the existence of the Creator, not the priest. I have found my own kind of faith: There is a God. The human mind cannot know what He is like."

Korczak felt his faith made very simple, but absolute demands on him: "Behave decently, and do good. Pray, not to ask things of God, but so as not to forget Him, because one should see Him everywhere."

In 1934 and again in 1936, Korczak visited Palestine to observe experimental education programs being developed on the kibbutz. The visits forced him to learn Hebrew and study the Torah for the first time in his life, as much out of intellectual curiosity as religious seeking (he would later write a children's bible, an academic book entitled *The Religion of the Child*, and a book on Moses as a child).

When he returned to Poland, the Third Reich was well in power next door, and had its eyes trained on Warsaw. Aware but unafraid of mounting anti-Semitism, Korczak began a famous radio program for children, called *The Old Doctor*. He continued to appear in juvenile courts, defending street children who were regularly arrested and sent to jail for unreasonably long sentences. But pressures from the anti-Semitic right wing eventually cost him all of his jobs except the directorship of the Jewish orphanage.

NEVER LEAVE YOUR POST

The German invasion in 1939 nearly forced the dissolution of the orphanage, but Korczak insisted it stay open. He smuggled in what food he could find, and rescued war orphans—some of whom had watched their parents slaughtered in front of them—from the street and brought them into the shelter. He refused to wear a Star of David armband when on his daily patrols for food and desperate children, despite the Nazi requirement that he do so.

When a Nazi officer asked where his armband was, Korczak answered, "There are human laws which are transitory, and higher laws which are eternal." He was beaten, arrested, and jailed for his disobedience. After several harrowing weeks in prison, a mysterious friend bailed him out and he returned to the children. Under the relentless onslaught of German atrocities in the streets outside and rampaging typhus among both children and adults, Korczak worked tirelessly—mounting plays and telling fairy tales—to keep the orphans cheerful and hopeful, and unaware of the horrors beyond their walls.

In his final months, as the Gestapo closed in, Korczak kept a diary that would later be as famous in Poland as Anne Frank's was in the Netherlands. The last of his Jewish students and fellow educators who were able to left Warsaw in the spring and early summer of 1942. According to Lifton, one friend asked Korczak, who was looking old and clearly ill, how he felt. "Like a butterfly," he replied. "A butterfly who will soon fly away to a better world."

Eyewitnesses would later reveal that Korczak was twice offered a reprieve by the Nazis—once at the train station, and again after his arrival at Treblinka—on the condition that he go to Germany and help reform the educational system for Aryan children. Both times he refused.

ACT NOW   www.korczak.com

♥ LEARN MORE

The Janusz Korczak Communication Center
Based in Munich, the site includes links to organizations associated with Korczak, as well as the complete text of Betty Jean Lifton's biography of Korczak, *The King of Children*.
Web site: http://korczak.com

The Janusz Korczak Living Heritage Association
Founded in 1971 by Michal Wroblewski, a former co-worker of Korczak's in Poland, the Association is affiliated with the Stockholm Teacher's College.
Web site:
http://fcit.coedu.usf.edu/holocaust/KORCZAK/default.htm
Email: wroblewski@medcellbio1.uu.se

Janusz Korczak
A German nonprofit Web site with excerpts of Korczak's plays and books, with biographical and scholarly resources.
www.janusz-korczak.de

The King of Children: The Life and Death of Janusz Korczak
by Betty Jean Lifton
Pan Books, 1989

A Hero and the Holocaust: The Story of Janusz and His Children
(for young readers)
by David Adler, illustrated by Bill Farnsworth
Holiday House, 2002

A Voice for the Child: The Inspirational Words of Janusz Korczak
by Janusz Korczak,
Sarah Joseph, ed
Thorsons, 1999

Ghetto Diary
by Janusz Korczak
Random House, 1981

DIETRICH BONHOEFFER

PROTESTANT THEOLOGIAN, NAZI RESISTER

"I f your opponent has a conscience, then follow Gandhi and nonviolence. But if your enemy has no conscience like Hitler, then follow Bonhoeffer." —Rev. Martin Luther King, Jr.

When Daniel Berrigan went underground in 1969, he brought with him one book: the autobiography of Dietrich Bonhoeffer, *Letters and Papers from Prison*. Bonhoeffer was a German professor, Protestant theologian, and Lutheran pastor who—with other prominent German religious figures like Martin Niemoller—served as the conscience of the German resistance movement during the brutal reign of Adolf Hitler.

In the early 1930s, Bonhoeffer warned against the encroaching fascism in Germany. But other church leaders were caving in, as the Nazis pressured the church and its pastors to pledge loyalty to Hitler and to remove the Old Testament from their Bibles (because of its connection to Judaism). Disgusted, Bonhoeffer left Germany and headed for England, where he stepped

ACT NOW www.dbonhoeffer.org

up his outspoken opposition to Hitler. While in London he became fast friends with Rev. George Bell, the Archbishop of Chichester, who was a prominent leader of the ecumenical movement and a close friend of Gandhi's.

Bonhoeffer returned to Germany and became involved in several underground missions to transport Jews out of the country and into Switzerland and England. His involvement in a conspiracy to assassinate Hitler led to his arrest at the hands of the Gestapo. He was ferried between concentration camps at Buchenwald and Flossenburg for a while, but was eventually convicted of conspiracy and hanged by order of Hitler himself. He was 39.

 # LEARN MORE

The International Dietrich Bonhoeffer Society
An international scholarly nonprofit organization dedicated to keeping the memory of Bonhoeffer alive. Includes books, videos, and links to other Bonhoeffer information.
www.dbonhoeffer.org/ibsinfo.htm

Dietrich Bonhoeffer: A Biography
by Eberhart Bethge
Fortress Press, 2000

Letters and Papers from Prison
by Dietrich Bonhoeffer
Macmillan Publishing Co., 1981

A Testament to Freedom: The Essential Writings of Dietrich Bonhoeffer
Geoffrey B. Kelly, editor
Harper San Francisco, 1995

The Cost of Discipleship
by Dietrich Bonhoeffer
Peter Smith Publications, 1983

MÁIREAD CORRIGAN MAGUIRE

CATHOLIC PEACE ORGANIZER

I t took a single horrible moment to turn Máiread Maguire into a lifelong crusader for peace. On August 10, 1976, a British army patrol was pursuing a suspected IRA gunman through the streets of Belfast, as Ann Maguire took a stroll with her three children, ages 6 weeks, 3 years, and 8 years. A shot rang out, and the suspect was instantly dead, but his car continued careening through the streets at speed.

The children died and Ann was critically wounded, all of them crushed under the wrecked getaway car with a dead man at the wheel. Máiread Corrigan Maguire lost two nephews and a niece that day. But out of that tragedy she also discovered the meaning of her own life. It would inspire her to dedicate herself to peace initiatives to end the interfaith violence known as "the Troubles." A week after the tragedy, Maguire and Betty Williams—a local housewife who had witnessed the children's deaths—organized a march for peace attended by 10,000

ACT NOW www.peacepeople.com

Protestant and Catholic women. They left from a Catholic neighborhood and marched through a Protestant enclave on their way to the gravesites of the Maguire children. IRA sympathizers screamed obscenities at them and threw stones, accusing them of sympathizing with the British. Still the women marched on. A week later, another march drew 35,000. By the end of 1976, peace marches inspired by Maguire and Williams were weekly events with half a million participants in Northern Ireland, England, and Ireland.

With Ciaran McKeown, Maguire and Williams founded the Community of Peace People that year, an organization dedicated to nonviolence, and set up programs to provide services to victims of the fighting. Maguire and Williams were awarded the 1976 Nobel Peace Prize for their efforts.

Maguire, a life-long Catholic and graduate of the Irish School of Ecumenics, has since traveled the world advocating nonviolent conflict resolution and building interfaith coalitions in conflict-rife regions. She has spoken out for the liberation of Tibet and East Timor, the end to sanctions in Iraq, and an end to the brutal corruption of the Burmese government.

She has advocated the ordination of women priests and lobbies the pope personally. Her well-publicized 1998 hunger strike at the jail where Philip Berrigan was being held for nonviolent protest against nuclear weapons caused the Bureau of Prisons to suspend his visitation rights for the rest of his 6-month sentence. The storm of publicity that followed forced the prison administration to back down.

In her "Open Letter to the IRA," Maguire wrote, "Wisdom means the tough decision to walk the path of non-violence. That risk of faith will take all your courage... In my own journey, I have come to know for certain that every human life is sacred and a gift. We have no right to take this gift of life from another, as they have no right to take our gift. I have come to know for certain that our first identity is not nationalist or unionist, but our humanity."

♥ LEARN MORE

Peace People
An interfaith volunteer organisation developing peace initiatives for Northern Ireland.
224 Lisburn Road
Belfast BT307NP
Northern Ireland
Tel:(44) (0)2890 663465
Email: info@peacepeople.com
Web site: www.peacepeople.com

PeaceJam
Bringing youth and Nobel Peace Laureate together in innovative educational programs.
www.peacejam.org

The Vision of Peace: Faith and Hope in Northern Ireland
by Máiread Corrigan Maguire
Orbis Books, 1999

Declaration of the Peace People

(read at the marches in 1976)

We have a simple message to the world from
this movement for Peace.

We want to live and love and build a just and peaceful society.

We want for our children, as we want for ourselves, our
lives at home, at work, and at play to be lives of joy and peace.

We recognize that to build such a society demands
dedication, hard work, and courage.

We recognize that there are many problems in our society
which are a source of conflict and violence.

We recognize that every bullet fired and every exploding
bomb make that work more difficult.

We reject the use of the bomb and the bullet and
all the techniques of violence.

We dedicate ourselves to working with our neighbors, near
and far, day in and day out, to build that peaceful society
in which the tragedies we have known are a bad memory
and a continuing warning.

❤ GET INVOLVED

The Corrymeela Community
An interfaith community of reconciliation founded in 1965 by Presbyterian Rev. Ray Davey, Corrymeela provided meeting space, residences, schools, shelter, and programs promoting peace for Catholics and Protestants.
8 Upper Crescent
Belfast BT7 1NT
Northern Ireland
Tel.: 028 9050 8080
Email: enquiries@corrymeela.org
Web site: www.corrymeela.org

Simon Weisenthal Center
An international Jewish human rights organization dedicated to promoting religious tolerance worldwide.
1399 South Roxbury Drive
Los Angeles, California 90035
United States
Tel.: (310) 553-9036
Email: information@wiesenthal.net
Web site: www.wiesenthal.com

International Interfaith Center
Founded in 1993 in Britain, the IIC is dedicated to interfaith cooperation and understanding.
Web site: www.interfaith-center.org

Peace Council
An international interfaith coalition of religious leaders (including Máiread Maguire, the Dalai Lama, and Bishop Desmond Tutu) founded in 1996 and dedicated to demonstrating "that peace is possible, and that effective interreligious collaboration to make peace also is possible."
Web site: www.peacecouncil.org

The Life & Peace Institute
Founded in 1985 by the Swedish Ecumenical Council, the Life & Peace Institute is an international and ecumenical center for peace research and action.
PO Box 1520
SE-751 45 Uppsala
Sweden
Email: info@life-peace.org
Web site: www.life-peace.org

MAN OF

THE TREES

RICHARD ST. BARBE BAKER

BAHA'I CONSERVATIONIST

He was surrounded by the Kikuyu warriors of central Kenya, a servant of the British throne insisting not only that they change their traditional methods of farming, but that they change their spiritual traditions. Richard St. Barbe Baker wasn't a Christian missionary, bent on converting the Kikuyu to Jesus. He was the world's first global environmentalist, and he was determined to begin his campaign to stem the destruction of the world's forests and repopulate the planet with new trees here, with the native tribesman of the African veldt.

As a new recruit in the British Colonial Service, he had been sent to Kenya to manage the forests. And so it was that he found himself explaining to an understandably skeptical Kikuyu tribe that their methods of farming would be their doom. As they slashed and burned the forests to make more and more room for their livestock and agricultural crops, the rich soil that had supported those crops for generations blew away with gathering speed, gradually turning the landscape to desert.

St. Barbe, as he came to be known, noted that the tribe had special dances of appreciation which they performed at the planting of the bean crop, at the reaping of the corn crop, and at nearly every other critical stage of their farming process. So he suggested a new tribal tradition, which he dubbed the "Dance of the Trees." The Kikuyu tribesmen would plant new

trees for each they cut, and celebrate with a dance to honor their god. Chief Josiah Njonjo was non-plussed at this white man suggesting a religious rite they had never heard of before. "That is god's business," Chief Njonjo said. "Yes, but if you cut all the trees, you don't give god a chance," replied St. Barbe.

On June 22, 1922, hundreds of Kikuyu gathered in a sacred place and took part in the first dance of the trees. A ceremony followed, in which 50 of the men swore themselves to the service of Kenya's forests, promising to protect existing trees and plant at least 10 trees every year for their lifetimes. The 50 men adopted the motto *twahamwe* meaning "pull together" in Swahili, and were dubbed *Watu wa Miti,* or "Men of the Trees" by their dumbfounded Masai neighbors.

In 1924, St. Barbe returned to England to found an international organization called "Men of the Trees," which carries on today as the International Tree Foundation. Today St. Barbe is credited with planting or inspiring the planting of as many as 1 trillion trees worldwide, in Kenya, Palestine, Canada, India, England, Nigeria, Australia, and New Zealand.

THE ROOTS OF PASSION

Richard St. Barbe Baker was born in 1889 in West End, near Southampton in Hampshire, the son of a rector in the local Anglican church. His father, Richard Baker, was also a nurseryman, and nurtured thousands of plants on his tiny farm. St. Barbe would later recall that as a boy he didn't play with toy soldiers, but rather imagined that the seedlings in his father's careful rows were regiments saluting him.

As a teenager, St. Barbe was obsessed with the natural world, and became a homesteader in Saskatchewan, Canada. When the University of Saskatchewan opened, St. Barbe was among its first 100 students. He spent summers earning his tuition in lumber camps, where he saw first-hand the devastation of clear-cutting. In the plains, he watched as prairies were turned to farmland and then to dust as native grasses and trees were removed and the soil blew away.

St. Barbe returned to Britain in 1913 to study divinity at Cambridge University. His plan was to emulate his father and become a man of God. But World War I broke out the following year, and St. Barbe abandoned his studies for a horse and a commission in the cavalry. Wounded twice in France, St. Barbe was discharged and awarded the Military Cross for valor. On his return to Cambridge, St. Barbe switched his studies to forestry. Upon graduation, he was posted to Kenya as the assistant conservator of forests for the colonial British government. Soon after, he met Chief Njonjo, and a global conservationist movement was born.

Awarded the Order of the British Empire for his conservation work late in his life, St. Barbe was admired widely, if looked upon as something of a nut. Almost every biographical sketch of him describes the man as "eccentric." Indeed, he was known for traveling around the world by rail and tossing tree seeds out the window, talking incessantly to friend and stranger alike about trees.

He is often wrongly credited with originating "tree-hugging" (its true origin is unclear), though he certainly practiced it regularly. After a particularly close call with his health, he prescribed himself a 2-minute hug twice a day with a Lebanese Cypress, a regimen he swore had curative powers. The American author Lowell Thomas once said he would not have been surprised to learn one day that St. Barbe had married a tree.

NATURE AS EXPRESSION OF THE CREATOR

When St. Barbe arrived back in England at the end of his posting in Kenya, he was invited to deliver a speech to a conference of world religions on the belief systems of the Kikuyu. During his speech, he recounted the founding of the dance of the trees, along with detailed descriptions of the native rites and rituals. When he stepped down from the podium, a stranger approached. "You are Baha'i!" she exclaimed. The woman was

"In the stillness of the mighty woods, man is made aware of the divine."
—Richard St. Barbe Baker

Claudia Stuart Coles, a prominent and enthusiastic messenger of the faith who explained the Baha'i tradition of conservation and respect for the dignity and interconnectedness of all life. St. Barbe, already a dedicated vegetarian and lay ecologist, was almost instantly won over.

Shortly after, he met with the Guardian of Baha'i faith to discuss the role of ecology and conservation in the observation of this still-new world religion. He learned that Baha'is hold that all living beings carry the spirit of the creator, and that it is therefore the responsibility of each Baha'i to live and teach accordingly. On the spot, St. Barbe pledged his faith. He would soon become one of the best-known Baha'is in the world. The Guardian of the Baha'i faith at the time, Shoghi Effendi, joined the Men of the Trees as its first lifetime member. Other lifetime members would include Franklin Delano Roosevelt and George Bernard Shaw.

REFORESTATION AS PRAYER

Planting trees was an act of faith to St. Barbe, more powerful and transformative than communion or baptism. "It is a high calling to which we are summoned—the peerage of the Men of the Trees—to be workers with God to protect our Elder tree Brethren who made it possible for the Creator to bring man on earth," he wrote in his book *The Redwoods* (George Ronald, 1960).

In 1929, St. Barbe traveled to Palestine, a region where skirmishes over the holy sites of three religions—Christianity, Judaism, and Islam—were becoming fiercer with each passing day. The Baha'i faith dictates that all religions are essentially the same and that the seeming differences are man-made, and so, near the holiest site of the Baha'i, St. Barbe founded a new chapter of the Men of the Trees with a special effort to include Christians, Jews, and Muslims in equal measure. St. Barbe saw the Men of the Trees as more than a conservation effort: Working together toward a common goal, the Men of the Trees were perhaps the first truly ecumenical peace project in what is now Israel.

St. Barbe, in 1940, recalled that his first visit to Palestine shocked him; the land was nothing like that described in the Bible he had studied as a child and in his brief foray into theology: "Sinai was not always a desert, but the tamarisks which once abounded and supplied manna to the wanderers in the wilderness are there no more," he wrote in *The Redwoods;* "The forests of Palestine have disappeared: Carmel and Lebanon are bare: no longer is balm found in Gilead, and there a rider, however reckless, may urge his mount without suffering the fate of Absalom."

His goal was to create a "Green Front" against the onslaught of the desert, thereby creating a greater area of livable land in the disputed region. It was a desperate and uphill battle. It also reflected the converse of St. Barbe's tree-planting verve: his deep distaste for deserts. Although modern ecologists argue that desert ecosystems are as vibrant and life-sustaining as forests, St. Barbe feared that deserts were taking over the world, and that "desertification" could spell the end for life on Earth.

The primary target in his war on sand became the Sahara, which was then expanding at a rate of 30 miles a year along a 30,000-mile front. In 1952 St. Barbe, convinced that the desert's growth was the direct result of deforestation, mounted the first of two expeditions into the driest, most lifeless reaches of the Sahara. Again, he allied himself with local tribesmen—

many of them from nomadic tribes who said they remembered trees and oases that had disappeared in their lifetimes. St. Barbe believed that a "green front" of trees 30 miles deep along the advancing front of the Sahara would impede its expansion into food-bearing regions of Africa. The project turned out to be a spectacular success in terms of media coverage and baseline research, but even the most enthusiastic tree-planting campaign has failed to slow the desert's steady march.

"A FRAGMENT OF EDEN"

In the early 1930s, St. Barbe Baker was invited to Northern California by local activists. They described to him by letter the trees of the region behemoths of inconceivable size and dignity, the cornerstones in a delicate ecosystem found nowhere else in the world. But industrialization had reached this remote spot, and the trees were being felled at a fantastic pace. Within a decade, they would all be gone, along with hundreds of plant and animal species found nowhere else.

When he arrived in the land of the coast redwoods, St. Barbe was transformed. He thought of H. Seton Merriman, who had once called a forest "a fragment from the Garden of Eden, coming to us directly from the hand of the Creator." The trees, which could reach well over 350 feet and live as long as 4,500 years, inspired him as no other had.

"Here is life unending...how can a man do justice or pay tribute to living things that reach toward immortality?" St. Barbe wrote. "They are as elder brethren, linking man with a cosmic life, without beginning or end."

ACT NOW www.internationaltreefoundation.org

St. Barbe helped found the Save the Redwoods League, which eventually set aside millions of acres for state parks in Northern California and protected some of the last virgin stands of trees from—including the Headwaters Forest where Julia Butterfly Hill made her famous tree-sit. But by the 1950s, it became clear that the state was easing logging restrictions and squeezing the watersheds that supported the delicate forests.

In 1958, St. Barbe went to Washington to speak at a Senate hearing on a wilderness bill then being considered. He heard ranchers, miners, loggers, and farmers argue for "multi-use" designations of federal lands. St. Barbe said "multi-use" was just a euphemism for "multi-destruction." Before he was called to testify, the slight, dignified Englishman rose quietly and left the Senate chambers without a word. "I felt I could no longer contribute even a note of sanity in a madly industrialized world, speeding to its doom," he recalled. In the 1970s, St. Barbe became an admirer and supporter of the Chipko movement in northern India. Women of the native Chipko tribe hug or chain themselves to native trees to prevent loggers from deforesting their land.

Richard St. Barbe Baker died in 1982 at the age of 93, just hours after planting a tree. He is buried in Saskatchewan, Canada. The Men of the Trees which changed its name in 1992 to the International Tree Foundation, today it has affiliates in Nigeria, Kenya, Scotland, Canada, Australia, the United States, and New Zealand (St. Barbe's adopted home).

♥ GET INVOLVED

International Tree Foundation
Sandy Lane, Crawley Down
West Sussex, RH10 4HS
United Kingdom
Email: itf@tree-foundation.org.uk
Web site:
www.internationaltreefoundation.org

Men of the Trees, Australia
PO Box 103
Guildford, Western Australia 6935
Tel: (08) 9250 1888
Email: contact@menofthetrees.com.au
Web site: www.menofthetrees.com.au

The Baha'i Institute for the Environment
34 Copernicus St., Ottawa
Ontario K1N 7K4
Canada
Tel.: (613) 233-1903
Email: abs-na@istar.ca

Man of the Trees: Selected Writings of Richard St. Barbe Baker
by Richard St. Barbe Baker with Karen Gridley
Ecology Action, 1989

JULIA BUTTERFLY HILL

PANTHEIST ENVIRONMENTALIST

T hose things of real worth in life are worth going to any length in love and respect to safeguard." —Julia Butterfly Hill.

Julia Butterfly Hill began looking for meaning in the redwoods of Northern California after she had nearly died in an automobile accident. "I experienced a deeply spiritual epiphany when I entered the majestic cathedral of a redwood forest," she writes in *One Makes the Difference*: *Inspiring Actions That Change Our World* (Harper Collins, 2002).

"I saw God as I had never believed possible—in the trees, in the ferns, moss, and mushrooms, in the air and water, birds and bears. I finally saw God with all of my senses, with all of who I am, from the inside out. God, both male and female. God, more than male, more than female. God of all life, in all of its forms... I had seen what was beautiful, profound, sacred."

ACT NOW   www.circleoflifefoundation.org

Today she is best known for a 738-day "tree-sit" in a huge coast redwood she named "Luna." Her peaceful protest not only saved the tree from the local timber mills, but called international attention to the dire plight of this last outpost of the ancient trees on Earth.

Luna was illegally cut a year after Julia's tree-sit ended. It is still standing, but may not survive the deep gash. Hill, meanwhile, has expanded her work to include social justice and environmental stewardship around the world through her Circle of Life Foundation.

 # LEARN MORE

Circle of Life Foundation
Sponsored by the Earth Island Institute, the Circle of Life Foundation is dedicated to saving ancient forests worldwide, as well as promoting sustainable lifestyles.
PO Box 3764
Oakland, California 94609
Tel: (510) 601-9790
Email: info@circleoflifefoundation.org
Web site: www.circleoflifefoundation.org

The Legacy of Luna
by Julia Butterfly Hill
HarperCollins USA, 2000

Save the Redwoods League
114 Sansome Street, Room 1200
San Francisco, CA 94104-3823
United States
Tel.: (415) 362-2352
Email: info@savetheredwoods.org
Web site: www.savetheredwoods.org

One Makes the Difference, Inspiring Actions that Change Our World
by Julia Butterfly Hill
HarperCollins USA, 2002

ROADS PROTESTORS

PAGAN EARTH DEFENDERS

The famous (or infamous) Roads Protestors of the U.K. have spent weeks in jail, been beaten and arrested repeatedly, and been vilified by townspeople and newspapers alike. Their actions include sitting in trees, chaining themselves to construction equipment, cementing their limbs into the road bed, chanting and singing, and generally mucking up plans by local governments and developers to plow new roads through the British countryside.

But these young activists see themselves as more than just troublemakers. Theirs is a higher calling from a generalized spirituality that suffuses all things, passing through generations and across religious, ethnic, and economic boundaries.

The protestors take up residence in trees that lie in the paths of new road-building projects, hoping to win delays or force construction to end. They don't usually win, but that's not so much the point.

"At the very beginning, earth spirituality was the dynamism that made it all happen," says one of the group's leaders, Josh Selby. "People moved onto the land to campaign more effectively, but this also connected them to each other, as a tribe, and reconnected them to nature and the spirituality of nature. It happened naturally, and was a spirituality felt collectively. It was the communal sense of spirituality that is very much to do with the spirituality of our connection with the earth, and that is something that has really been lost in our culture. Because that has been lost we've become capable of destroying the earth, of destroying sacred and beautiful places and treating other creatures as if they have no value. It was this connection with the spirituality of nature that gave people the inner strength to risk their lives in defense of the earth."

SULAK SIVARAKSA

BUDDHIST ENVIRONMENTAL ORGANIZER

On a March day in 1998, as the sun reached its zenith, Sulak Sivaraksa and some 50 students and activists were taken from their encampment in the Huay Kayeng forest by Thai police.

For nearly three months, the activists had placed their bodies between the bulldozers and this strip of pristine rainforest in Thailand's Kanchanaburi province.

Now the forest would be cleared to make way for the Yadana gas pipeline—a project built by the oil companies Unocal and Total that has been marked by allegations of forced labor, environmental devastation, and wholesale displacement of indigenous peoples. "We do not want gas at the expense of our neighbor's blood," insisted Sivaraksa after his arrest.

Sivaraksa, probably Thailand's most prominent and outspoken social and environmental activist, had been at odds with the Thai authorities many times over the years. When the

ACT NOW   www.sulak-sivaraksa.org

LEARN MORE

Sathirakoses-Nagapradeepa Foundation
Founded by Sulak Sivaraksa in 1968, the
Foundation is an umbrella network for five
sister organizations founded by Sulak
Sivaraksa: the Thai Inter-Religious
Commission for Development, Santi Pracha
Dhamma Institute, Wongsanit Ashram,
International Networks of Engaged
Buddhists, and Spirit in Education
Movement.
Wongsanit Ashram
PO Box 1, Ongkarak, Nakornnayok
26120 Siam (Thailand)
Tel.: 66-37-333183-4, 66-1-8036442
Email: ashram@cscoms.com
Web site: www.sulak-sivaraksa.org

Buddhist Peace Fellowship
PO Box 4650
Berkeley, California 94704
United States
Tel.: (510) 655-6169
Email: bpf@bpf.org
Web site: www.bpf.org

International Network of Engaged Buddhists
Founded in Thailand, the INEB brings
together Buddhist clergy and laypeople for
"grassroots dharma action around the
world."
P.O. Box 19, Mahadthai Post Office
Bangkok, 10206
Thailand
Tel.: 662-433-7169
Email: ineb@ipied.tu.ac.th
Web site: www.bpf.org/ineb.html

**Seeds of Peace: A Buddhist Vision for
Renewing Society**
by Sulak Sivaraksa
Parallax Press, 1991

**Loyalty Demands Dissent: Autobiography of
an Engaged Buddhist**
by Sulak Sivaraksa
Parallax Press, 1998

mlitary regime was ousted in 1973, his work helped spark the student movement that led to their overthrow. After the bloody coup of 1976, in which hundreds of students were killed, he was forced into a two-year exile. His book *Unmasking Thai Society* prompted a 1984 arrest for defaming the monarchy—though after a four-month trial and an international campaign on his behalf, the king intervened to have the charge withdrawn. In 1991, the military junta charged him with defaming both the king and the commander of the armed forces, and Sivaraksa spent another year in exile; returning to face trial a year later, he was finally acquitted in 1995.

Sivaraksa has combined incisive intellectual work with constant grassroots organizing, founding more than a dozen rural development projects, international organizations, and Thai NGOs that explore alternative models of sustainable and spiritually based development.

A leading exponent of socially engaged Buddhism, Sivaraksa believes Buddhists must stop focusing on individuals and take on the system. "Meditation alone is not sufficient," he explained in *Turning Wheel* magazine, "because people suffer so much. One must also act; one must do what one can."

❤ GET INVOLVED

Heifer International

A nonprofit organization rooted in the Christian tradition, Heifer International aids impoverished families worldwide by giving them livestock and training them in environmentally sound sustainable farming methods.
PO Box 8058
Little Rock, AR 72203
United States
Tel.: (501) 907-2600
Web site: www.heifer.org

Future Harvest

With the dual purpose of bringing peace and ending hunger this global charity funds research in sustainable farming and helps implement the results in poor communities.
PO Box 238
2020 Pennsylvania Avenue, NW
Washington, DC 20006-1846
United States
Tel.: (202) 473-1142
Email: info@futureharvest.org
Web site: www.futureharvest.org

Global Witness

Nominated for a joint Nobel Peace Prize in 2002, this non-governmental investigative group works to gather and disseminate evidence of the link between environmental exploitation and human-rights abuses, particularly in Africa and Asia.
PO Box 6042
London, N19 5WP
United Kingdom
Tel.: +44 (0)20 7272 6731
Fax: +44 (0)20 7272 9425
Email: mail@globalwitness.org
Web site: www.globalwitness.org

Cousteau Society

Through exploration and education, the membership-supported, nonprofit Society aims to protect the "Water Planet" and improve the quality of life for present and future generations.
870 Greenbrier Circle, Suite 402
Chesapeake, VA 23320
United States
Tel.: (800) 441-4395
Email: cousteau@cousteausociety.org
Web site: www.cousteausociety.org

ACKNOWLEDGMENTS

PRAISE, PROPS, AND PAEANS

First and foremost, the greatest thanks must be reserved for Anita Roddick OBE, whose passion for the subject, patience with the rest of us, and tenaciousness in getting this book out are the reasons you now hold it in your hands. Anita is an inspiration to know and work with, and I am blessed to have been given the opportunity to write this book for her.

My deepest gratitude to my valued friend and co-conspirator Cal Joy, who picked up this project mid-stream and shepherded it through unknown and sometimes frighteningly mysterious territory, doing all the hard, dirty, behind-the-scenes work willingly and without complaint. I am indebted to Justine Roddick for her willingness to listen to my panicked ramblings about minuscule details at all hours and counsel me back to sanity. But this book would truly not have been possible without the a magnanimous patience, goodwill and uncanny organizational skills of the remarkable Karen Bishop.

I extend my most heartfelt appreciation to my indispensable editor Kate McKinley, who could make (and to some extent has made) a lucrative career out of preventing me from looking quite as stupid as I am able; and to Michelle Pilley and Alex Fisher who were knowledgeable and insightful midwives when the book was in its earliest stages, and who, with Mark Durham, contributed to the research and composition of several chapters. Special thanks go to the miracle workers at Wheelhouse Creative Ltd. in London, especially designers Rob Robinson and Steve Chambers, for another spectacular job.

The process of writing this book moved and inspired me in unexpected ways, and I owe the people within it an incalculable debt of gratitude for expanding my own spiritual understanding. Thanks especially to those who made time to speak to me at length, including Rev. Mel White, Neta Golan, Fr. Roy Bourgeois, and John Trudell.

Many people offered advice and recommendations for this book that proved invaluable, among them Dana Powell, Max Carter, Melody Ermachild, Amy Ray, Lanell Dike, Redwood Mary, Faye Brown, Audrey Howard, Satish Kumar, the staff of the National Labor Committee, the staff of Bolerium Books in San Francisco, and many others.

This book is an effort to present a collection of inspirational stories about a few magnificently brave individuals who put their lives where their hearts and souls are. I know there are dozens—perhaps hundreds, even thousands—of equally brave souls out there who are worthy of inclusion among these ranks; I do not mean to imply by their absence that they are any less deserving of our recognition, respect, admiration, or emulation.

Brooke Shelby Biggs, 2003

PHOTOGRAPH CREDITS

INTRODUCTION

5   Muriel Bouquet

CHAPTER ONE

11   AP Wide World
13   AP Wide World
15   Michel Laurent/AP Wide World
18   AP Wide World
21   CORBIS
22   Daniel Berrigan by Richard Drew;
      Phillip Berrigan by Ted Mathias;
      antiwar protestors by Daniel Hulshizer.
      All courtesy of AP Wide World.
29   Trident missile by Phil Sandlin/AP Wide World;
      all other images courtesy of Trident Ploughshares.
31   AP Wide World
33   Siddiqi Ray/AP Wide World

CHAPTER TWO

37   Fr. Roy Bourgeois (upper right) courtesy of
      School of the Americas Watch. All other images by
      Elliot Minor/AP Wide World
38   Bernard Kolenberg/AP Wide World
41   All photos courtesy of AP Wide World: Hugo
      Banzer by Sandra Boulanger; Pinochet by Paul
44   Infographic by Steve Chambers. Photo (bottom) by
      Elliot Minor/AP Wide World.
48   Photo by Linda Panetta/
      SOA Watch Northeast www.soawne.org
50   Ric Francis/AP Wide World
51   AP Wide World
53   Victor Ruiz/AP Wide World
54   Luis Romero/AP Wide World

CHAPTER THREE

59   Eric Risberg/AP Wide World
60   Photodisc
63   AP Wide World
66   AP Wide World
69   Old woman by Don Ryan; young girl by Pat
      Carter. Both courtesy of AP Wide World.
70   AP Wide World
73   Moises Castillo/AP Wide World
76   Chad Harder/AP Wide World

CHAPTER FOUR

81   Russell Boyce/REUTERS
82   AP Wide World
85   David Crosling/AP Wide World
88   Penny Tweedie/CORBIS
90   Steven Dupont, Baci/CORBIS
93   Rob Griffith/AP Wide World
94   Charles Perkins photo courtesy of CORBIS;
      protest photo by David Gray/CORBIS; "Sorry"
      photo by Rob Griffith/AP Wide World; John
      Howard photo courtesy of AP Wide World/ News Ltd.
97   Rick Rycroft/AP Wide World
98   Canberra Times/AP Wide World
100   Dario Lopez-Mills/AP Wide World

CHAPTER FIVE

105   CORBIS
106   CORBIS
109   AP Wide World
112   Upper left photo of migrant workers by Dorthea
      Lange. All images courtesy of AP Wide World.
115   Leon Trotsky courtesy of Hulton-Deutsch
      Collection/CORBIS; Ho Chi Minh and Karl Marx
      courtesy of AP Wide World.

116   White House image courtesy AP Wide World;
      candle image and collage by Wheelhouse Creative.

117   AP Wide World

119   Adele Starr/AP Wide World

120   Barry Sweet and Sakuma
      /AP Wide World

123   CORBIS

124   AP Wide World

CHAPTER SIX

129   AP Wide World

130   Photos courtesy of AP Wide World

133   Infographic by Steve Chambers/
      Wheelhouse Creative.

136   S.S. Harrison/AP Wide World

139   Photo courtesy of Satish Kumar

140   Images courtesy of AP Wide World

144   Ajit Kumar/AP Wide World

CHAPTER SEVEN

151   David Zalubowski/AP Wide World

152   All images courtesy of AP Wide World

155   All images courtesy of AP Wide World

158   Photo illustration by Steve Chambers/
      Wheelhouse Creative.

161   Gary C. Knapp/AP Wide World

164   James A. Finley/AP Wide World

166   Photo courtesy of Jose Cabezon

169   AP Wide World

171   AP Wide World

173   AP Wide World

CHAPTER EIGHT

177   Heidi Levine/Sipa Press-Paris

178   Lefteris Pitarakis/AP Wide World

181   Adel Hana/AP Wide World

182   Charles Dharapak/AP Wide World

185   All images courtesy of AP Wide World. Barricade by
      Marco Di Lauro; olive picker by
      Jacqueline Larma; soldier by Gadi Kabalo.

186   Khalil Hamra/AP Wide World

189   Adel Hana/AP Wide World

190   David Guttenfelder/AP Wide World

193   Photo courtesy of theAmerican Friends Service
      Committee

194   Gadi Kabalo/AP Wide World

197   AP Wide World

199   Photo courtesy of RAWA

CHAPTER NINE

205   Janusz Korczak Communication Center

206   Young boy courtesy AP Wide World. All other
      images by Wheelhouse Creative.

211   Julien Bryan/AP Wide World

212   Collage by Steve Chambers/Wheelhouse Creative.
      Schoolhouse photos by Pilar Capurro/AP Wide
      World and Kevin Fleming/CORBIS.

215   AP Wide World

218   International Network on Personal Meaning

220   Eduardo Verdugo/AP Wide World

222   AP Wide World

223   Paul McErlane/AP Wide World

CHAPTER TEN

229   Photo courtesy of the
      International Tree Foundation

230   CORBIS

233   Wheelhouse Creative

236   Doug Thuron/AP Wide World

238   Rich Pedroncelli/AP Wide World

240   ShaunWalker/AP Wide World

243   Photo courtesy of Adrian Arbib

244   AP Wide World

get **informed,**
get **outraged,**
get **inspired,**
get **active!**

AnitaRoddick.com

AnitaRoddick.com is eclectic, full of personal essays, quirky links, breaking news, and activist information. Updated regularly, Anita's site is vital and well-regarded within the weblogging community.

Whether she is filing dispatches from the Amazon rainforest, or soliciting tongue-in-cheek spoofs of corporate logos, or pillorying world leaders for their war-like ways, Anita's website is a peek into the mind of a woman, an entrepreneur, an activist, a grandmother, a curious and concerned global citizen. It is full of joy and passion, outrage and information.

A REVOLUTION IN KINDNESS

The concept of kindness is often perceived as a passive, squishy, weak quality. We must reclaim this word and the meaning of it from those who would suggest that it is merely a quality we should "practice randomly." Kindness should not be random; kindness should be deliberate and bold and aggressive. Real kindness is active and alive.

WHAT WE NEED NOW IS A REVOLUTION IN KINDNESS

This moving, unexpected, and eclectic collection of essays by celebrities, soldiers, political prisoners, down-and-outs, doctors, philosophers, activists and musicians, is part mosaic and part manifesto. Taken together, these intimate self-portraits make the joyful argument that kindness is not just something to be practiced randomly, but a truly revolutionary idea that really can change the world.

ISBN: 0-9543959-1-3   Retail Price: UK £7.99, US $12.95
(Volume, non-profit, and educational
discounts available. Please call for pricing.)
From U.S. telephones: 1-800-423-7087   From U.K. telephones: 0800 018 5450
Or visit www.AnitaRoddick.com

TAKE IT PERSONALLY

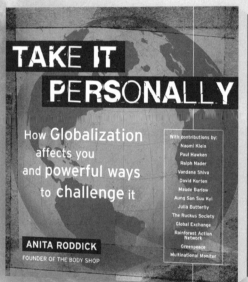

A revolution is taking hold across the globe. Daily news reports tell us of the sweatshops that produce Gap clothing, the child labor that goes into Nike running shoes, and the deplorable demands that are put on the agricultural workers who bring us Starbucks coffee. Through the work of reporters, photographers, underground investigators, and the testimony of people working in inhuman conditions, accounts of the sad and shocking working and living conditions of people around the world have provoked a humanitarian response.

How Globalization affects you and powerful ways to challenge it

A vibrant collection of photographs, essays, montages, and quotes on the driving issues behind globalization from impassioned writers and activist organizations, this is the definitive handbook for the average consumer who wants to learn about the issues and make informed choices.

US-ISBN: 1-57324-707-3 UK-ISBN:0-00-712898-3
Retail Price: U.K. £12.99, U.S. $24.95 (Volume, non-profit and educational discounts available. Please call for pricing.)
From U.S. telephones: 1-800-423-7087
Or visit www.AnitaRoddick.com